The Integral Being: A Qualitative Investigation of Highly Sensitive Persons and Temperament-Appropriate Careers

Tracy M. Cooper, Ph.D.

A Dissertation Submitted to the Faculty of

The California Institute of Integral Studies

in Partial Fulfillment of the Requirements for the Degree of

Doctor of Philosophy in Transformative Studies

California Institute of Integral Studies

San Francisco, CA

2014

The Integral Being: A Qualitative Investigation of Highly Sensitive Persons and Temperament-Appropriate Careers

Copyright © 2016 by Tracy Cooper

ISBN-13: 978-1537562261

Invictus Publishing, llc
2303 South 16th Street
Ozark, MO 65721

Author's website: www.drtracycooper.com

Printed by CreateSpace, Charleston, SC
Printed in the United States of America
Published by Invictus Publishing, llc
First printing: September 2016

DEDICATION

Several people have played key roles in inspiring me to move forward in this endeavor. First and foremost my wife, Lisa, who believed in me and inspired my return to school almost six years ago. This is *our* accomplishment!

Secondly, my beautiful children: Peter, Ally, Indianna, Ben, and my step-children: Christopher, Micheal, and Caitlin, for whom I set this example of scholarship, service to others, and proof that setting big goals and persisting does pay off. Follow your curiosity and be your most authentic selves.

Thirdly, I dedicate this to my Mother who always believed in me and whose self-less example of unconditional love, charity, and sacrifice clearly exemplify the "better angels of our nature."

Lastly, I dedicate this to my Father who passed away so long ago and never had the chance to see this accomplishment, but which I no doubt believe he would be thrilled and elated by.

TABLE OF CONTENTS

CERTIFICATE OF APPROVAL

I certify that I have read THE INTEGRAL BEING: A QUALITATIVE INVESTIGATION OF HIGHLY SENSITIVE PERSONS AND TEMPERAMENT-APPROPRIATE CAREERS by Tracy M. Cooper, and that in my opinion this work meets the criteria for approving a dissertation submitted in partial fulfillment of the requirements for the Doctor of Philosophy in Transformative Studies at the California Institute of Integral Studies.

Michael A. Raffanti, Ed.D., Chair
Adjunct Professor, Transformative Inquiry Department

Joanne Gozawa, Ph.D.
Associate Professor, Transformative Inquiry Department

Ted Zeff, Ph.D.
California Institute of Integral Studies

Tracy M. Cooper
California Institute of Integral Studies, 2014
Michael A. Raffanti, Ph.D., Committee Chair

THE INTEGRAL BEING: A QUALITATIVE
INVESTIGATION OF HIGHLY SENSITIVE PERSONS AND
TEMPERAMENT-APPROPRIATE CAREERS

ABSTRACT

This qualitative study investigated the lived experiences of highly sensitive persons (HSPs) to better understand the way they experience careers. Sensory processing sensitivity (SPS) is the underlying personality trait and is present in approximately 20 percent of the population, equally distributed across gender and racial lines. SPS is considered a non-normative personality trait in some Western societies and subcultures. Thus, many HSPs experience difficulty finding an appropriate match between innate temperament and career.

This qualitative research perspective employed semi-structured interviews with 35 participants recruited through social media web sites and snowball sampling. Participants in the study were primarily from the U.S., but also from five foreign countries. Participants were chosen based on answers to a recruitment questionnaire and Elaine Aron's HSP Self-Test. Major findings reveal a complex, interwoven dynamic interplay between nine major themes: (1) empathy, (2) childhood's influence, (3) self-care, (4) a rich inner life, (5) creativity, (6) high sensation-seeking, (7) the sociological perspective, (8) the experience of work, and (9) the integral being. The significance of this study is that it is the first of its kind to investigate this topic in a systematic, scientific manner.

ACKNOWLEDGEMENTS

First, I would like to express my sincere appreciation to my Dissertation Committee Chair, Michael Raffanti, and to my committee members, Joanne Gozawa and Ted Zeff. Michael provided the right focus on rigorous qualitative research, combined with an openness to the heuristic process. That orientation toward flexibility and emergence was necessary in this study because it is the first of its kind. Joanne brought a sense of sincere, deep authenticity to the committee that I resonated with and I appreciate her quiet strength. Ted brought the outsider expert point of view and contributed his decades of experience counseling highly sensitive persons to this study. His contributions during the proposal defense were invaluable in ensuring this study would be balanced and useful to a wide audience. I would also like to acknowledge Elaine Aron for her early help in conceptualizing this study.

My path was never certain and always filled with ambiguity. I acknowledge the early validation in my Ph.D. program provided by Robin Robertson, who believed in my writing ability. I also acknowledge the significant contributions of many of the professors at the California Institute of Integral Studies, especially Allan Leslie Combs, Daniel Deslauriers, Alfonso Montuori, Constance Jones, Linda Shepherd, Jennifer Wells, and, of course, Michael Raffanti. Their collective wisdom and embodiment of what it means to be a Ph.D. has provided me with needed role models. I deeply appreciate their willingness to embrace and welcome me into the academic fold.

This path has also been a shared one with the cohort of 2011 and I must express my deep appreciation and love for the community of friends and colleagues that has been created. Jay Beeks, Melani Farmer, Oren Cox, Miyoko Nida, Thomas Gallagher, Toni Aspin, Kim MacQueen, Terry Teaters, Karla Hankes, Sandy Baba, Sara Chou, Aran Baker, Nermin Soyalp, Sherill Lambruschini, Carol Simpson, Shelly Gupta, Rick Wilson, Gabrielle Donnelly, Maria Firmino-Castillo, Ashanti Jackson, Gabi Fernandez-Borsot, Mary Clare Foecke, Miriam Garay Foronda, Kim Gralnick, Claudia Hall, Cheryl Johnson, Claudette Anderson, and Nick Walker, thank you for your authenticity, kindness, warmth, love, and support. I cherish our beloved community!

I would also like to thank my colleague Leslie Scholar for suggesting I read Elaine Aron's book *The Highly Sensitive Person* at the beginning of my journey in 2011.

CHAPTER 1: INTRODUCTION

Statement of the Problem

Highly sensitive persons (HSPs) represent approximately 20% of the total population and possess a personality trait known as sensory processing sensitivity (SPS). This trait is distinguished by depth of processing of all stimulation, a propensity for feeling easily over aroused as compared to others, high empathy and emotional reactivity, and sensitivity to subtle stimuli (Aron & Aron, 1997). For HSPs finding a career that, both, integrates and honors their unique trait may prove problematic.

Many HSPs may grow up unaware of why they react very strongly to noises, smells, textures, and the energy of others. Indeed, many may feel as if there is something "wrong with them," as they compare themselves to the dominant cultural ideals, which often include being highly extraverted, paying little attention to inner physical and emotional needs, and withstanding a constant barrage of stimulation. In the working world HSPs may experience greater difficulty than others in finding a career that works with their unique temperament due to cultural bias in favor of extraversion, basic psychological needs being unfulfilled, and interpersonal issues (Jaeger, 2004).

Peer-reviewed research addressing the real-world problem of HSPs and careers has not been conducted before. Thus, this study is the first of its kind and represents an initial first step toward reconciling this need.

1

Significance of the Study

This study seeks to reveal the broad range of variables that may influence the way HSPs experience careers in an attempt to better understand the difficulties, as well as the possibilities for growth and development inherent in HSPs. The lack of useful research may lead to diminished realization of human potential and perpetuation of suffering for those HSPs who lack adequate self-awareness about their trait and their unique emotional needs (Leavy, 2011). It is my hope that this study will serve as an entry point of understanding for HSPs and non-HSPs alike with the goal of increased awareness of the gifts and needs of HSPs.

In a time of global cultural metamorphosis HSPs may have a significant role to play in intuiting the way forward as we seek to reimagine our lives and reinvent ways of being that honor community, inclusion, and the development of each individual's inherent potential (Slater, 2009). HSPs often deeply intuitive nature exemplifies a "canary in the coal mine" relational perspective in which serious societal issues may be identified early. This holds the potential for great benefit to society if these individuals can be integrated into corporate, government, and spiritual spheres of influence while respecting the psychosocial needs of HSPs.

This study is of great importance to the millions of HSPs around the world who find themselves searching for an authentic way of being and to societies that desperately seek tacit knowledge and leadership on profound and deep levels of human consciousness. This study specifically investigated the way HSPs experience careers inclusive of gender, culture, and social class with the hope that participants would reveal a broad range of variables for further investigation.

Personal Relationship to the Topic

I have always known intrinsically that I was different, more sensitive to all experience than others, and tended to feel and think deeply. However, I did not have terminology for my lived experience until I discovered the work of Elaine Aron and Arthur Aron in 2012. After thoroughly reviewing their research papers (Aron & Aron, 1997; Aron, Aron, & Davies, 2005; Aron, E., 2006; Aron, E., 2010; Aron, Aron, and Jagiellowicz, 2012) I reflected on the role of sensory processing sensitivity in my own life and concluded the effects have been pervasive. I have experienced great difficulty in finding a career that works for me given that I feel deeply, require an environment with autonomy, creative challenge, meaningful work, and connectedness, and yet prefer to work in small groups or alone. Being a male HSP has exacerbated the issue because in the traditional view of masculinity men are expected to be competitive, strong, risk-taking, aggressive, and powerful, as well as display sexual prowess, be emotionally distant, and be dominant over women (Kimmel & Kaufman, 1994). This rigid view of what males are "supposed" to embody denies the complexity of my lived experience.

At the age of 43 I realized the endless treadmill existence of unfulfilling work opportunities necessitated that I completely rethink how I approached life. Existing within a working environment where I felt a constant mismatch between my capabilities, needs, and talents bred a sense of depression and hopelessness I could no longer tolerate. Key to this new approach to life would be following an organic path of inquiry in an open-minded manner wherever it led. Fortunately, the path led me to greater and greater realizations about the contextual factors that had controlled and influenced my life to date.

Finally arriving at the heart of my experience in life as a HSP I determined to better understand how this personality trait predisposed me toward a deep need for authenticity in work and life. I felt this could benefit not only my life, but the lives of many others, HSP and non-HSP alike. The deeper I began to understand what it means to be a HSP the more questions I had. I wanted to know about aspects of myself like my deeply empathetic side, highly creative disposition, love of learning, and my need for new stimulation. I began to realize I would never find adequate answers in self-reflection only and knew I needed to learn from the experiences of others like me. This study parallels a twin need for self-knowledge as well as a desire to create new knowledge with the potential of solving real-world problems.

CHAPTER 2: LITERATURE REVIEW

Overview

Studies on people with sensory processing sensitivity [SPS] — or the more commonly known phrase highly sensitive persons [HSPs] — are relatively few in number with no significant addressing of the real-world issues of HSPs and careers except the work of Jaeger (2004). This review critically examines the research from a transdisciplinary viewpoint seeking to transcend disciplinary silos and incorporate useful knowledge from several domains. Though the research into SPS is ongoing, the twenty percent of the population with SPS may experience ongoing issues with careers, which this review attempts to identify and explicate.

Definition of Highly Sensitive Person

Based on the research of Aron and Aron (1997) and Aron, Aron and Jagiellowicz (2012) highly sensitive people are the 20 percent of the worldwide population who process experience more deeply — fueled by emotion — with no difference in the sense organs themselves. Highly sensitive people subjectively process experience before acting, may be overstimulated by sensory input, are aware of subtleties before others, are highly creative, intuitive, empathic, and conscientious (Aron, 2010). Seventy percent of HSPs are introverted, while 30 percent are extraverted; approximately one third of HSPs experienced unhappy childhoods predisposing them to depression, anxiety, and other psychological issues; approximately two thirds of HSPs experienced happy childhoods and may be no different than others except in terms of their sensitivity; lastly, HSPs tend to be more deeply affected by positive and negative experiences than others due to the depth of cognitive and emotional processing (Aron & Aron, 1997). Jaeger (2004), described HSPs as intense, which seems to be an apt descriptor given the above definitions.

SPS is an innate personality trait that is often confused with introversion and shyness. Introversion, while also a trait, is primarily a measure of sociability; shyness is a learned behavior based on past negative social experiences (Aron, 1997). Taken as a whole we see a group of individuals who think deeply and feel deeply, with a trait that is not widely understood or accepted as normative (Aron, 2010). Introverted HSPs, due to their quiet demeanors and propensity for thinking before acting may appear to others as complex, aloof, unfriendly, and even unintelligent (Bendersky & Shaw, 2013). Extraverted HSPs may appear similar to other extraverts, yet may be overwhelmed by too much stimulation and need to withdraw and recharge. This may lead others to believe they are neurotic or fragile in spite of their sociability (Aron, 2010). A last group of HSPs exist called high sensation seekers (Jaeger, 2004). These individuals actively seek out stimulation and crave the novelty of new and exciting activities. HSPs with high sensation-seeking tendencies may find themselves simultaneously pulled toward stimulation, yet repelled by too much. Aron (2010) referred to high sensation seeking as having one foot on the brake and one on the gas meaning the craving for stimulation is equally as strong as the need to moderate its intake. In a work situation one might readily foresee how each type of HSP would fit into a particular niche based on characteristics of each position; however, the reality is more complex.

Historical Timeline of Research

HSPs are not a new phenomenon. Carl Jung (1913) wrote about what he termed innate sensitiveness many times, most notably in the Fordham lectures just prior to his break from Freud. Jung espoused the view that the libido was not the primary basis of neuroticism. Jung's view was that the constitutional trait of innate sensitiveness was inborn and observable even in early infancy. Jung (1921) equated sensitivity with neuroticism and valued sensitive individuals as embodying a rich and overflowing interior life, which he felt was lacking in Western civilization due to its largely materialistic orientation. Jung felt there was something to be learned for all of us from those who are inwardly oriented.

Jung (1913) judged there to be a fundamental difference in individuals who processed stimulation inwardly. He described it as psychic assimilation (as cited in Campbell, 1971), rather than continually looking to the object for interpretation, as in extraversion. In Jung's view, all kinds of events leave a powerful, lasting impression on sensitive individuals and this is rooted in an inborn sensitivity. For Jung sensitivity is the root cause of neurosis, not libido, and is present in about a quarter of the population (Jung, 1913, para. 398). This percentage was later confirmed by Aron and Aron (1997) and Kagan (1994). Jung (1921) described those with sensitivity as having to lead a highly individual life because of their very different nature. Jung was the first to use the terms introversion/extraversion, but not the last in conceiving of the subjective processing of experience. Eysenck's (1957) view of introversion – which was convoluted with sensitivity for many decades – was one of inhibition and excitation, with introverts seeking to avoid overstimulation.

Eysenck (1981) introduced the concept of a psychobiological basis for introversion, but downplayed the role of impulsivity and emphasized low sociability as a primary identifier of the trait. Gray (1981) brought impulsivity back and added anxiety (1985) in a model establishing the psychobiological basis for the trait based on two areas of the brain: the behavioral activation system [BAS], and the behavioral inhibition system [BIS] (1991). Gray's revised model (McNaughton & Gray, 2000) envisions the BIS as the mediator between impulses and fear. Inhibition in this sense is a preference to process information before proceeding. These distinctions were further enhanced by Cloninger (1987) with the addition of a behavioral maintenance system which acts to revisit what has enabled reward or eased suffering in the past; however, the success of the Big Five Model (McRae & John, 1992), with sociability as the primary distinction between introversion-extraversion, has dominated the discourse.

The Big-Five Taxonomy

The post-war environment of the mid-twentieth century

was a time of boundless optimism, a time when many thought it was time for grand, new theories to explain everything. In the view of many researchers the Allied victory in World War II was evidence of capability; thus, the feeling existed that there was little researchers could not do. Psychologists embarked on creating grand theories to explain what hitherto had been piecemeal models. The Big-Five taxonomy was an attempt to distill the bewildering array of personality trait scales into a common language (John & Srivastava, 1999) and create a new model that could effectively simplify the large number of specific conceptualizations.

The Big Five were developed through a lengthy analysis of natural language terms that people used to describe themselves or others (Allport & Odbert, 1936; Baumgarten, 1933; Klages, 1926). Allport and Odbert's list comprised 18,000 terms people used to delineate individual behavior (as cited in John & Srivastava, 1999). Norman (1967) postulated that individuals can be described by enduring traits, internal states, physical states, activities, effects on others, roles, and evaluations of conduct (as cited in John & Srivastava, 1999). Chaplain, John and Goldberg (1988) developed a prototypical model in which states were seen as externally caused and temporary, while traits were stable and internally caused. Cattell (1943, 1945a, 1945b) reduced Allport and Odbert's list to 4,500 terms with 35 variables, later reducing it further to 12 personality factors.

Later research by Fiske (1949) and Tupes and Christal (1961) found there were five "strong and recurrent factors."

These became the Big Five and represent the broadest level of abstraction summarizing more distinct personality characteristics within each (John & Srivastava, 1999). The Big Five are usually labeled as extraversion, agreeableness, conscientiousness, neuroticism, and openness (Goldberg, 1981). Additional work by Goldberg (1990) and Goldberg and Saucier (1996) further validated earlier findings regarding the invariability of the Big Five even when rotated and subjected to different models of factor extraction (John & Srivastava, 1999). Now that the lexical tradition had been reasonably settled researchers wanted an integrative framework with which to study personality.

Costa and McCrae's (1985, 1992) questionnaire-based approach (the Five-Factor Model) to studying personality complemented Goldberg's lexically-based research, but the acceptance of the Big Five still depends on which Big Five is in question with any of the five aspects open to interpretation based on the researcher (John & Srivastava, 1999). Costa and McCrae's Five-Factor Theory of Personality (McCrae, 1992; Costa & McCrae, 1993; Costa & McCrae, 1998) has become the leading exemplar of a theory of personality, though they do not claim it is a theory, rather an attempt to construct a theory based on current understanding of personality (McCrae & Costa, 1999). At least 16 meta-analytic studies of personality as related to job performance have been performed indicating the prevalence of Five-Factor Theory (Barrick & Mount, 2003).

It is important to acknowledge that Five-Factor Theory has been challenged by Block (1995); Wiggins (1968), who suggested two factors; Eysenck (1991), who posited three factors; Hogan (1986), with six factors; Jackson (1984) with seven factors; Hough (1992) with nine; and Hough (1998a, 1998b) with eight factors. Thus, there is no consensus in the literature indicating this attempt at a grand theory has achieved its goals, other than in the broadest, most abstract way. Researchers have yet to create an integrative framework that appreciates that individuals are differentiated and dynamic beings living in complex social environments (Hogan et al., 1997). Further, Barrick and Mount (1991) demonstrated that the relation between the five factors of personality vary according to career and job criteria; thus, certain job classifications would benefit more from a particular combination of personality traits than others. Employers, however, have latched onto personality testing, believing that personality equals job performance (Barrick & Mount, 2003). Employers' increasing use of personality surveys to prescreen applicants may make securing the job difficult for HSPs who do fit a particular profile.

There is no consensus that testing for broad personality traits is better than testing for narrow traits (Rothstein & Goffin, 2006). This seems to raise the issue that employers may be relying on personality questionnaires based on incomplete knowledge of the research and may not be the best way to relate personality traits to job performance. In fact, there is only one factor that has been found to be reliable in predicting job performance: conscientiousness (Barrick & Mount, 1991; Barrick, Stewart & Mount, 1998). HSPs are typically very high in conscientiousness (Aron, 2010) and may feel social pressure to perform based on avoidance of social disapproval (Arkin, 1981; Elliot & Thrash, 2002; & Higgins, 2000).

Companies and organizations have embraced personality testing prior to hiring candidates at ever-increasing rates (Beagrie, 2005; Erickson, 2004; Heller, 2005). This may be particularly difficult for introverted HSPs, who represent 70 percent of HSPs, (Aron & Aron, 1997). The 30 percent of HSPs who identify as extraverts may experience fewer problems with pre-employment and subsequent personality screening because they would likely seem to fit the criteria employers seem to desire, namely, positive affect and extraversion (Alarcon, Eschleman & Bowling, 2009).

HSPs in the Workplace

The workplace is often a hierarchical structure with status accorded based on certain personality characteristics, favoring extraverts who demonstrate dominance, aggressiveness, and enthusiasm (Anderson, John, Keltner & Kring, 2001; Hogan & Hogan, 1991; Anderson & Kilduff, 2009; Barry & Stewart, 1997). Those who do not display these qualities are accorded lesser status, with less expected of them (Bendersky & Shah, 2012). For introverted HSPs, who are often perceived as quiet and reserved, this would seem to represent a major issue in terms of advancement, engagement, and career satisfaction. But, what of the 30 percent of HSPs who are extraverted? Do they risk being classed as neurotic because they seem to act like other extraverts socially, yet withdraw at times to recharge? And what of high sensation seeking HSPs who thrive on novelty? The workplace is a complex environment for HSPs, one in which expectations of extraversion may put them at a disadvantage for advancement, status, and career potential. What has changed in the postmodern age about occupations to cause a shift toward extraversion?

Wilcock (1993) defined occupation as a mechanism reflecting use of individual capacity in ways that allow achievements of value to the community. Occupation prior to the post-modern age was primarily rooted in subsistence with a necessary and significant engagement of capacities, later becoming more complex due to technological innovations deemphasizing full engagement. Advancements in technology have removed much of the former drudgery, yet people still have a need to engage their capacities to maintain and develop themselves. This is a key point as HSPs may feel the need for meaningful work and full engagement more than others, due to their temperament. Maslow (1968) emphasized that the use of capacities is necessary for growth and they clamor to be used until they are fully engaged. What happens when individuals are unable to fully engage their capacities or develop themselves in ways they feel they should? As complex beings (Aron & Aron, 1997) do HSPs fall into the trap of underutilization of capacity and subsequent boredom?

Martin, Sadlo and Stew (2006) described boredom as an inability to focus attention combined with negative attitudes. Do HSP's become bored on the job because of negative affect, as the Five-Factor Model would have us believe (McCrae, 1992; Costa & McCrae, 1993; Costa & McCrae, 1998)? Aron, Aron, and

Jagiellowicz (2012) found no correlation regarding HSPs and negative affect except a likelihood in the one-third who experienced an unhappy childhood. However, that claim is subject to scrutiny because of what Dabrowski (1964) described as the third force or the ability of individuals to make life choices that diverge from expected paths. Is the inability to focus attention mentioned by Martin et al. related to occupational deprivation? Csikszentmihalyi (1975, 1992a, 1992b) postulated that individuals who believe their abilities to be higher than the challenges of the task may become bored. HSPs may fall into this category if they believe their abilities are being underutilized and may lead to burnout. This may be true of anyone, but especially of HSPs because they process and reflect on experience more deeply (Aron & Aron, 1997). Beyond boredom related to underutilized potential there is also the issue of burnout on the job.

Underutilization of capacity, coupled with stressful conditions can lead to worker burnout (Fernet, Gagne, & Austin, 2010). Alarcon et al. (2009) compared personality factors against several measures, including the Five-Factor Model (Costa & McCrae, 1992). Alarcon et al. (2009) examined burnout from an individual standpoint addressing each aspect of the Five-Factor Model and finding that positive affect, negative affect and emotional stability all exhibited strong correlations with emotional exhaustion. One might expect negative affect and emotional stability to correlate well with emotional exhaustion, but not positive affect. Alarcon, et al. (2009) concluded this result was unexpected and may indicate that positive affect and extraversion are different variables. Thus, a HSP may exhibit a positive affect and not be extraverted.

Though Alarcon et al. do not recommend weeding out individuals who test as prone to burnout, they do advocate a more careful matching of employees to job based on personality and suggest some employees may benefit from stress-reduction training. HSPs may or may not be susceptible to emotional exhaustion, burnout, boredom, and underutilization of capacities, but they are all possible routes for further research to help determine why HSPs experience difficulty finding a temperament-appropriate career and in what circumstances they experience an appropriate fit.

What about the basic psychological needs of HSPs? Do they differ based on HSPs depth of cognitive and emotional processing (Aron et al. 2012) and what role does need satisfaction play in career happiness? For the answer I looked to self-determination theory [SDT], (Deci & Ryan, 2000).

SDT emphasizes the role of basic needs satisfaction in optimal functioning of the individual (Deci & Ryan, 2000) with intrinsic need satisfaction valued over extrinsic needs. Intrinsic motivations are considered to be stronger with regard to providing basic psychological needs satisfaction because when individuals engage in activities that follow their own inner interests they perceive them to be internally caused and, thus inherently more fulfilling (Deci & Ryan, 2000). SDT is a three-pronged theory with autonomy, competence, and relatedness representing the most significant factors imbuing well-being, psychological flexibility, and vitality (Ryan & Frederick, 1997;

Ryan, Deci & Grolnick, 1995). When an individual's need for autonomy, competence, and relatedness is thwarted through the social world the individual functions at a less than optimal level exhibiting substitute fulfillment and compensatory activities (Deci & Ryan, 2000). Seligman's (2006) learned helplessness — the giving-up reaction — may become a factor for those who believe negative events are personal, pervasive, and permanent. HSPs are particularly prone to rumination based on explanatory style because of their subjective internalization of experiences. Pessimistic HSPs may be the most vulnerable to consciously expecting the worst, which can lead to depression.

SDT and learned helplessness, as applied to HSPs, seem to imply a psychological cost will be incurred if basic psychological needs are not met and explanatory style becomes pessimistically oriented. Anxiety, depression, alienation, and inner conflict are a few of the ramifications for HSPs, as well as undermined potential and lack of psychological energy (Broeck, Vansteenkiste, De Witte, Soenens, & Lens, (2010). Maslow (1968) argued that capacities if not fulfilled will become sources of illness and instability. This argument suggests several research questions. First, do HSPs experience basic psychological needs satisfaction in their careers? Second, what experiences and insights do HSPs report in their search for temperament-appropriate careers? There are likely a number of other questions that arise related to variables including the role of gender, culture, education level, and socioeconomic background, but these are a few that seem immediate.

Sensory Processing Sensitivity

The work of Elaine Aron and Arthur Aron forms the bulk of the research performed to date into SPS with their first major study taking place in 1997. Their initial foray intended to distinguish the personality characteristic of high sensitivity that comprised 50 percent of their patients. Proposing a new model of sensory processing sensitivity [SPS], Aron and Aron (1997) focused not on any difference in the sense organs themselves, but rather on the way that sensory information is processed in the brain.

Pulling from the extensive research on introversion indicating differences in the way input is processed Aron and Aron (1997) suggested a greater capacity for reflection, attention, and discrimination. Further, they cited work on sensory sensitivity by other researchers, most notably Thomas and Chess (1977), who studied low sensory threshold in children, Fine (1972, 1973), who espoused the view that there are differences in sensitivity based on studies of color and weight discrimination tasks, and Mehrabian (1976, 1991) and Mehrabian and O'Reilly (1980), who connected arousability to sensitivity or openness. Establishing tentative links between Gray's model of anatomical differences in the brain and research related to SPS, including Kagan (1994), Gunnar (1994), and Patterson and Newman (1993), Aron and Aron (1997) proposed a model of SPS that emphasized that a large minority of individuals may possess a greater psychobiological preference for input over output, for reflection over action, and greater consciousness of self and environment.

To research this, Aron and Aron (1997) conducted a series of seven studies designed to better understand the basic characteristics of self-described HSPs. Searching for a core pattern among those basic characteristics Aron and Aron (1997) sought the relation of those items to introversion and emotionality, possible sub-groups of HSPs, and SPS's relation to childhood experience. Replicating results based on Eysenck (1981) and Mehrabian's (1976) work, Aron and Aron (1997) developed the HSP scale and compared it to Eysenck's EPI E scale and the Big Five's measures of introversion and emotionality (Goldberg, 1990).

Results from these studies indicated that the construct of SPS is partially independent of introversion and emotionality. SPS is a unidimensional construct; SPS is not introversion and emotionality combined; one third of HSPs reported experiencing unhappy childhoods (especially males) with higher scores on introversion and emotionality; and the newly developed HSP scale is reliable with convergent and discriminatory validity (Aron & Aron, 1997). A later revision by Aron, Aron, and Davies (2005) reflected the importance of emotional reactivity in SPS with emotionality now more deeply embedded into the construct. Jaeger (2004) describes it as intensity with HSPs reacting emotionally to a greater degree than the situation may warrant. This fits the current view of Baumeister, Vohs, DeWall, and Zhang (2007); Koolhaas, et al. (1999); Schjolden and Winberg (2007); and Groothius and Carere (2005) that similar processes involving depth of processing of stimulation exist in the non-human world. SPS, or something resembling it, has been found in at least 100 species to date (Aron et al. 2012). This seems to indicate that SPS in a certain percentage of many species is part of an overall differentiated survival strategy.

Aron et al. (2012, 2014) refined the definitions of SPS further to include the role of cross-over interactions and depth of processing as coming closest to capturing SPS further reinforced by FMRI studies showing greater activation in brain areas related to making connections between information coming into the brain and information already in the brain and in general awareness across the brain (particularly the insula). Aron et al. elevated emotional reactivity's role in promoting thorough processing of experience (as put forth by Baumeister et al., 2007) and related negative affect to negative experiences in childhood for one third of HSPs. Additionally, Aron et al. postulated that HSPs high in SPS may be more sensitive to cultural acceptance of SPS, while potentially being misclassified as shy or neurotic when SPS may be the underlying trait misattributed as shyness or neuroticism.

Objections to Sensory Processing Sensitivity

Sensory processing sensitivity, as Aron and Aron (1997) envisioned the construct, is by no means accepted across the board. There are objections to various aspects of Aron and Aron's 1997 study and a lack of further sensitivity research is probably attributable to the prevalence of the Big Five in contemporary research circles. Additionally, personality traits are observable and, thus measurable, but this tells us nothing of the inner workings of the person. We are reliant on self-reports for information in that regard with self-report bias always remaining as a factor for some.

Smolewska, McCabe, and Woody (2006) questioned one of the central measures developed by Aron and Aron (1997): the HSP scale. Challenging the notion that the HSP scale measures a unidimensional construct, Smolewska et al. (2006) instead found a three-component structure featuring ease of excitation, aesthetic sensitivity, and low sensory threshold. Evers, Rasche, and Schabracq (2008) reported similar findings as Smoleska et al. (2006) regarding the three-component structure; however, they do admit their subscale scores indicate a general cohesive construct.

Smolewska et al. (2006) additionally compared the HSP scale to the Five-Factor Model and found a correlation similar to Aron and Aron (1997), plus a correlation to openness, which Aron and Aron had expected, but did not find in their sample (1997). Aron et al. (2012) postulated that the lack of correlation to the other three factors may be largely due to the Five-Factor Model's description of introversion as lack of positive affect, while sensitivity is actually high in positive affect and only partially related to introversion. What Aron et al. (2012) did find was that HSPs reporting happy childhoods were as likely as the rest of the population to possess a positive affect, but those HSPs reporting unhappy childhoods were more likely to resemble the Big Five introversion construct of negative affect. This distinction is important because it points out the need for further refinements to the Five-Factor Model and the need to avoid the homogenization of HSPs.

Alternate Conceptualizations

Martanuska (2012) cited Strelau's (1996) conception of sensory sensitivity [SS] as a divergent theory dissociated from emotion, instead focusing on the awareness of stimuli and imparting a regulatory mechanism to sensory sensitivity (Strelau, 1996, 2009; Strelau & Zawadski, 1993, 1995). In this view, sensory sensitivity serves to regulate the amount of sensory information an individual receives versus the amount perceived (Martanuska, 2012), thus sensory sensitivity becomes an ability (or behavioral characteristic) as opposed to a central property. This view portrays sensory sensitivity as a more rudimentary, more elementary theory (Martanuska, 2012). If Strelau offered us a different take on sensory sensitivity by disavowing the role of emotion, Dabrowski (1964) provided a comprehensive theory of development quite unlike Aron and Aron or Strelau.

Dabrowski (1964, 1967, 1972) and Dabrowski and Piechowski (1970) proposed a theory of personality development postulating that personality is not fixed. Rather personality is shaped by each individual through a process called positive disintegration (1964). The Theory of Positive Disintegration [TPD] refers to the development process by which an individual experiences negative emotions or dissatisfaction with lower-order biological needs and societal norms and reintegrates at a higher level of being (Dabrowski, 1964).

Dabrowski believed that many people have "developmental potential," based on what he terms overexcitabilities. Overexcitabilities [OE] are higher-than-average responsiveness to stimuli, likely due to a heightened sensitivity in the nervous system. Dabrowski viewed these overexcitabilities as hereditary endowments, thus not present in every individual to the same degree. Individuals with overexcitability experience reality in a more multifaceted manner with more intense processing of stimulation (Dabrowski, 1972).

In the theory of positive disintegration overexcitabilities constitute five distinct categories: psychomotor, sensual, intellectual, imaginational, and emotional (Falk, Manzanero, Miller, 1997). Psychomotor OE is distinguished by curiosity, high energy, and restlessness; sensual OE involves high sensitivity in the senses of smell, touch, hearing, feeling, and seeing; intellectual OE is exemplified by a love of learning and ability to analyze and synthesize concepts; imaginational OE reflects a heightened play of the imagination where creativity and fantasy abound; and emotional OE applies to sensitive individuals who process experience deeply, are empathic, experience complex emotions, and experience intense feelings (Mendaglio, 2008).

Similar to Aron et al., (2012) Dabrowski emphasized the role of emotion, and that the experience of negative emotion plays a key role in primary disintegration leading to potential reintegration at higher levels (Mendaglio, 2008). For Aron et al., (2012) emotion is the fuel that causes depth of processing. The role of emotion in influencing personality development is further substantiated by Brandstatter and Eliaz (2001), Izard and Ackerman (2000), and Eisenberg, Fabes, Guthrie, and Reiser (2002).

Dabrowski's theory (1964) seems to point out a specific population of individuals with highly sensitive nervous systems; who feel more deeply; may be highly creative; may exhibit a heightened sense of curiosity and love of learning; may experience deep, complex emotions, and for whom life is often complex with the development of an autonomous, self-directed, morally-driven realization of what it means to be truly human as the tentative goal (as cited in Mendaglio, 2008). Dabrowski's theory is on a grander scale and encapsulates a broad theory of development, whereas Aron and Aron's work (1997) has primarily focused on description and delineation of HSPs.

Ernest Hartmann (1992, 2011) offered one last alternate way of looking at the construct of sensitivity, albeit in broad terms. Hartmann envisions the mind as separated by boundaries that may be thick or thin (using the extreme of both to illustrate the model) with thick boundaries defined by clear focus; no in-between states of consciousness; clear separation of past, present, and future; division between thoughts and feelings; non-ambiguous sexual identity; and black and white thinking (Hartmann, 1992). Thin boundaries are defined by high intake of sensory stimulation; awareness of thoughts and feelings combined; experience of in-between states of consciousness (daydreaming, fantasy); awareness of past blended with present; inclusive sexual identity; and transient group membership status (Hartmann, 1992). Hartmann emphasized that most people fall somewhere in between with thick boundaries serving to keep thoughts neat, clear and focused, while thin boundaries permit divergent, novel thinking (as cited in Medneck, 1962). Hartmann (2011) contended that boundaries represent a defensive and possibly adaptive, pervasive dimension of personality.

In this case, Hartmann's theory seems to be describing individuals much like HSPs with high intake of sensory stimuli, heightened awareness, and openness to divergent thinking (Hartmann, 2011). Interestingly, Aron and Aron (1997), Dabrowski (1964), and Hartmann (2011) all explicitly state that HSPs, those with OE, and those with thin boundaries (respectively) may be highly creative or open to divergent thinking. Further, descriptions of creative people seem to mirror attributes of HSPs. Csikszentmihalyi (1996), described creative individuals as those who developed a sensitive nervous system where novelty stimulates pleasure centers in the brain (the high sensation seekers Aron describes?); may be caring and sensitive; love to make connections between and across bodies of knowledge; possess a genetic predisposition for a sensitive nervous system; are open to experience, thus recognizing novelty; are psychologically androgynous, expressing introversion and extraversion at the same time; exhibit complexity of the mind; shape events to suit their purposes; and are able to focus intently, yet often are at rest and quiet.

These parallels appear to suggest that HSPs are creative by innate predisposition, yet no research exists in this regard. If

HSPs are creative by nature, how does possessing a creative predisposition affect career choice and later satisfaction? Can one be innately creative – able to pick up on subtleties before others; possess highly sensitive nervous systems; be both intuitive and empathic; and conscientious (Aron & Aron, 1997) – and experience career satisfaction in many of the highly specialized roles common in the U.S.? Csikszentmihalyi (1996) said creative individuals become funneled toward specialization by the demands of their roles. He described this as the most difficult paradox of creativity. This review is not suggesting that all HSPs are creative and experience difficulties in careers due to their creative nature, but this may be one significant aspect leading to dissatisfaction in careers.

Discussion

In this transdisciplinary literature review I have presented SPS as researched and illuminated by Aron and Aron, described how occupational science viewed the way people experience careers, examined the development of the Big Five and the Five-Factor Model, and offered various theories that seem to refer to a similar group of sensitive individuals. I have contrasted Aron and Aron's findings with those of Strelau, Hartmann, and Dabrowski. Taken as a whole all seem to point to a large minority of the population that possess a personality trait that makes their lives more challenging, yet potentially more rewarding and original, than others might experience. I have outlined the literature concerning basic psychological needs, boredom, and creativity as I intuit they apply to HSPs. In doing so I have attempted to provide snapshots of the current research literature and reveal gaps where new research needs to take place.

This search found that no significant research studies exist examining the difficulties HSPs experience in finding temperament-appropriate careers, except for Jaeger (2004). At present the focus seems to lie on the Five-Factor Model, which does not explicitly address HSPs. Aron and Aron have demonstrated that HSPs who reported happy childhoods do not resemble the neurotics possessing negative affect described in the Five-Factor Model (Aron & Aron, 1997). This leaves the 20 percent of the population who self-describe as HSPs out of the mainstream research community. A transdisciplinary literature review, by its' nature, is oriented toward finding solutions to real-world problems.

Additional research could explore the relation between careers and HSPs to determine if HSPs fit better into particular categories of work based on introversion/extraversion and other tendencies like high sensation seeking and optimism/pessimism. Other variables such as gender, cultural and familial background, socioeconomic status, religiosity, etc. all merit further research with the promise of further explicating the ways HSPs experience temperament-appropriate careers.

CHAPTER 3:

METHOD

This chapter details the methodology chosen for this study with an account of the exact procedures followed for participant recruitment and selection, interviewing, and data analysis processes. As advised by Maxwell (2005) and Seidman (2013) I allowed the research problem itself to determine my choice of method. Since my interest was in knowing the discreet experiences of other HSPs I chose to utilize a qualitative, semi-structured interview process.

The qualitative paradigm within which this study operates is fundamentally a multifaceted, iterative, spiral approach that allows for a continual reformulation of the research problem as the study progresses (Creswell, 2003). In order to understand how HSPs experience careers it is necessary that I explore each participant's point of view, the context within which they live, and the meanings each hold for their experiences. Qualitative research is uniquely oriented toward just this goal and is especially appropriate when the variables are not known and need to be identified (Seidman, 2013). I felt these factors helped qualify qualitative research as an appropriate perspective. Further, this study is also rooted in transdisciplinarity.

Transdisciplinarity is a problem-generated, holistic, synergistic approach to research that places the problem itself at the center of the research process irrespective of disciplinary silos and is intended to solve real-world problems (Leavy, 2011). My perspective is also informed by the theoretical contributions of creative inquiry, an outlook that is based on intrinsic motivation, independence of judgment, tolerance of ambiguity, complexity of outlook, and openness to new experience (Montuori, 2008). In creative inquiry the inquirers' own passionate interests become the focus of scholarship. Combined together transdisciplinarity and creative inquiry form an attitude and approach towards inquiry that is holistic, synergistic, emergent, contextualizing, connecting, and is intended to build useful, new knowledge (Leavy, 2011). Epistemologically transdisciplinarity and creative inquiry assume that how we know what we know should not be confined to disciplinary silos, rather it should be open to the creative process inherent in all of us and allowed to engage with the researcher's attempts to make sense of the world (Montuori, 2008). Combining qualitative research with transdisciplinarity and creative inquiry provides the open, flexible, researcher-centered attitude necessary to address the real-world problems many HSPs experience.

Participant Recruitment and Selection

The study was designed to include a range of 20-40 participants. The exact number to stop at was based on saturation, or the point at which no significant new information is being provided by participants (Lincoln & Guba, 1985; Rubin & Rubin, 1995). Participants were recruited from several social media groups dedicated to HSPs on Facebook and additional participants recommended by my external committee member, Ted Zeff. I selected participants partially based on responses to a participant assessment questionnaire (Appendix A) I designed to gather basic demographic information and situate the participants in a sociocultural context. This questionnaire asked questions like: What is your age? What country are you from? What is your highest level of education? What is your gender? What is your current career? How many careers have you had since age 18? This information was used to ensure selection of participants was balanced by gender, age, and culture.

Along with the questionnaire I asked each participant to complete Elaine Aron's HSP Self-Test (Appendix B) in order to ensure each participant was a HSP other than by self-identifying. The HSP Self-Test has been shown to have convergent, discriminant, and reliability as a valid construct (Evers et al., 2008; Smolewska et al., 2006), thus I felt comfortable using it as an instrument.

Once I received HRRC approval (Appendix C) to conduct my study I posted identical invitations (Appendix D) in the social media groups I previously determined were good participant pools. I measured worthiness by noting the number of members in each group and by monitoring the daily activity level in each group. The most active groups seemed to hold the most promise for interested participants, thus I posted in those groups. A later effort to recruit participants utilized snowballing, which is a technique whereby initial contacts refer new participants (Biernacki & Waldorf, 1981). Several participants who were involved in social media groups, such as meetup.com, sent announcements to the members of their respective groups. Interested participants then contacted me through email.

Once participants returned the completed HSP Self-Test and I determined they seemed to be a good fit for the study I emailed them an informed consent form (Appendix E), along with a participant bill of rights (Appendix F), and scheduled the interview at a convenient time for each participant. I asked each participant to pick a time when they would not be distracted by household or work activities so they would be more relaxed and likely to provide good information.

Each interview was scheduled to last approximately 90 minutes and was conducted through Skype video messenger service or by telephone in some cases. A few days prior to each interview I sent each participant a list of sample questions (Appendix G). I based furnishing questions in advance on several factors: one, HSPs are deep thinking individuals who prefer to consider their answers before having to give them, and, two, the types of questions I wanted to ask required a significant amount of introspection and self-reflection in order to be able to provide significant, well-considered information.

Interview Protocol

I designed the following interview protocol as a loose guide to use in each interview with the aim of allowing each participant significant flexibility in revealing meaningful experiences.

1. Can you tell me about your background?
    a. Where you are from?
    b. Where you grew up?
    c. How many people are in your family?
    d. Were your parents supportive of you?

2. What was your childhood like?
    a. Your school experience?
    b. What kind of interests did you have as a child?
    c. Did you know in some sense that you were a sensitive person?
3. What were you first experiences with work?
    a. What kinds of jobs did you have?
    b. What kinds of issues emerged in your first jobs if any?
    c. How did you envision having a career at that point in your life?
    d. In what ways has that vision changed now?
4. Can you tell me about each of the jobs you have had?
    a. What did you like about each one?
    b. What did you dislike about each one?
    c. Why did you decide to leave?
5. Looking back how do you feel being a HSP affected your choice of jobs?
    a. Has it been harder to find a job that works for you because of being a HSP?
    b. Has being a HSP been helpful in your working life? In what ways?
    c. What role did the physical working environment play for you?
    d. Were there any things about where you worked, like lights, cold/hot, cramped spaces that bothered you?
    e. Were you affected by any interpersonal issues in your work? In what ways?

6. What kind of work do you like to do?
    a. What kinds of things matter to you in a job?
    b. What motivates you?
7. What role has being a highly sensitive male played for you? (where appropriate).
    a. Has finding the right career been harder because you are a highly sensitive male? In what ways?
8. How are HSPs viewed in your culture? (where appropriate).

I designed each question to be open-ended to allow a space for the participant to respond in a way that felt most appropriate.

Data Collection

After receiving approval from the HRRC interviews soon ensued. Prior to the official beginning of the interview phase of the study I conducted two trial runs of the interview questions with a person who did not participate in the study, but self-identified as a HSP. I allowed the same individual to interview me using the same questions so I could better relate to how participants related to each question and understand the efforts involved in formulating answers. This trial run was of great value in informing the research demeanor I needed to present. The interview process in qualitative research is intentionally free-flowing, but requires that the researcher listen very deeply and create a safe space for participants to feel comfortable enough to divulge intimate details of their lives.

Deep listening is a technique that incorporates the

listener in mind and body acting from a calm, focused center allowing the known and unexpected to come forth while maintaining a tolerance for ambiguity and the heuristic process (Rome & Martine, 2010; Watkins & Lorenz, 2002). Prior to each interview I spent a few minutes decompressing in quiet and opening my consciousness to attend to the present moment. The space I attempted to create was a calm, focused one that allowed for a free-flowing exchange between participant and researcher.

At the beginning of each interview I reminded participants that each interview was completely anonymous with no identifying information appearing in the final dissertation and that they were free to request any information provided be removed. Additionally, I spent a minute or two in casual conversation with each participant and asked if I could answer any questions about the structure or purpose of the study. My intent was to acclimate, both, myself and the participant to each other in a relaxed, pleasant manner before asking any serious questions. Each interview lasted between 60-90 minutes and was audio recorded utilizing two handheld, digital recording devices. The second unit was for a backup copy of the interview in case of any technical mishaps. At the conclusion of each interview I asked participants if they had any questions for me about the study itself, to allow them a chance to decompress from the interview and return to a calm state before ending the call.

After each interview I created research memos (Maxwell, 2005) noting important points about participant experiences and my impressions regarding the interview process. Researcher memos are a powerful tool for researchers to record fleeting thoughts for later referral and represent an integral component in the ongoing data analysis of the study.

Interviews were transcribed by a trained transcriptionist. I transcribed two interviews personally and decided, due to the length of time required to accurately type each transcript, that my time would be more efficiently utilized in conducting additional interviews given the study's time frame. There were some difficulties finding an appropriate transcriptionist due to issues of availability and reliability. The individual I settled on fortuitously was willing to provide her skills to aid the study, since she is a HSP herself. I required her to sign a confidentiality agreement (Appendix H) stating that she would hold all information in strict confidence and destroy her files after I verified receipt of each complete file. I felt comfortable with this arrangement because none of the participant files were identified by name and none of the participants are local or known by the transcriptionist, thus confidentiality was fully maintained. The transcriptionist stated that she had enjoyed making a contribution to what she felt was an important study and had learned a great deal about herself in the process.

Data Analysis

Following receipt of each transcription I initiated a recursive or spiral coding process that consisted of four cycles of first cycle coding and a second cycle consisting of pattern coding. Prior to beginning I decided to print hard copies of approximately 15 transcripts. My reasoning was based on uncertainty regarding my ability to focus on a computer screen for extended periods, plus a desire to physically manipulate and participate in the coding process. Each transcript was set up with the interview verbiage on the left half of the page, leaving the right half for codes. Saldana (2009) advised that researchers should trust their instincts and bear in mind that coding is primarily an interpretive act. In the first cycle I read each entire transcript to refamiliarize myself with the interview, but did not start coding at this point. Reading through the corpus lessens the likelihood of unexpected surprises later in the process due to lack of understanding of what Saldana (2009), termed the "big picture." This deep reading represented the entirety of the first cycle.

In the second cycle I used ink highlighters to bracket important passages with different colors for each type. Several types of codes were initially identified to comprise my initial coding process, though following Saldana's advice I kept the inclusion of each code dependent on its ability to generate useful information. My initial codes were holistic, in vivo, and descriptive and were chosen based on a pilot study conducted in 2012 in which I learned the value of remaining close to the participant's own words. Holistic seemed especially appropriate because there was such a large amount of data, the time for analysis was limited, and I had a general idea of what to look for in the data, though I remained open to divergent information.

In the third cycle of my coding process I assigned codes to the highlighted phrases, passages, and words. These codes, chosen for their capacity to summarize as well as reduce, were notated in the right column. Some codes were used repetitively and began to suggest patterns, such as self-care seemed an obvious choice with numerous examples of HSPs mentioning the need to care for themselves in a variety of ways. Explicating the exact self-care methods suggested further that self-care needed to comprise an entire theme. In this way I allowed the data itself to inform the emerging big picture.

For the fourth cycle of coding I created a separate document for each transcript listing the themes that had emerged in earlier cycles and sorted the codes generated in the third cycle into their respective themes. In some cases individual codes fit more than one theme and I included them wherever they seemed to fit and provide a generative quality. An example of this was self-knowledge or the increasing understanding of participants that they are HSPs. This code fit, both, self-care and inner life and reflected the complexity of lived experience. At the conclusion of coding for the 15 printed transcripts I felt I had developed a streamlined coding process and coded the remainder of the transcripts as computer files.

The process I developed included replacing descriptive coding with initial coding, using more in vivo codes to remain closer to the participant's words, and less hesitation about the process itself. My four cycle process repeated for the remaining transcripts, with the only change being that I created my profile document utilizing more of the phrases and vernacular of each participant, rather than descriptive codes. I found that the more I immersed myself in each transcript the less I wanted to confuse the emerging picture with outside words that told me little of what the participant had actually said. Thus, entire phrases were sorted into categories. There are several advantages to this approach: one, it provides easy reference for the researcher to be reminded of significant events in each participant's life, two, remaining close to the participant's words allows the summary to retain the freshness and vitality of each participant, and finally, there is less confusion and less time spent trying to understand what a general code might mean. For example, "I began to practice yoga and found it to be transformational in my life," is more meaningful than simply "self-care." My coding process began with splitting data and ended with lumping as I learned what I was looking for, understood what had meaning, and could better identify the words, phrases and passages that would be of most value.

For the second cycle of coding I reviewed all 35 summary documents noting themes that appeared in more than one theme and in more than one question. I then created a meta-document with each theme listed in order of relative importance. I established a hierarchical order based on frequency of mention, both, within a question and across questions. The themes loosely follow the types of questions I asked in the interviews, but several emerged from questions designed to elicit insight, but not necessarily the level of response I expected to receive. One instance of this is the self-care category, which became one of the major themes in this study. The high sensation-seeking theme emerged entirely unplanned. I did not specifically recruit participants who possess the separate traits sensory processing sensitivity and high sensation-seeking. The presence of these individuals in the study is an unexpected addition demonstrating qualitative research's inherent flexibility, particularistic focus, and capability for generating new knowledge with a direct bearing on the topic under consideration.

I found Saldana's explanation of the coding process as "decorating a room; you try it, step back, move a few things, step back again, try a serious reorganization, and so on" (Abbott, 2004 as cited in Saldana, 2009) to be extremely accurate in describing the flexible approach required to distill these data into themes. As coding progressed it became obvious certain types of codes appeared repetitively across questions, eventually suggesting entire themes. Furthermore, Maxwell (2005) suggests qualitative research can help the researcher better understand the context within which participants act, thus I felt that in order to better inform my central research question of how HSPs experience careers I needed to understand both macro and micro-level processes that influence behavior. In this sense, my coding process identified themes explicating complex interactive processes that partially influence or determine behavior and attitudes toward careers. Lastly, I submitted a copy of the nine themes I identified to members of my committee for their review and suggestions. None of the committee members suggested any revisions or changes.

CHAPTER 4:

RESULTS

In this chapter I describe the participants in the study and include a narrative presentation of basic demographic characteristics including age, gender, culture, educational level, marital status, and careers represented by the participants. This information is provided to add context to the participants I chose for this study and further explicate the complex nature of their lived experiences. The intent of this study was to reveal the broad range of variables associated with a non-homogenous group of individuals dispersed throughout geographic regions of the U.S., with a small sample from other cultures. Additionally, I delineate the nine themes that emerged as a result of the coding process and provide a discussion of each theme with accompanying quotes from participants. I end with a summary of chapter four: results.

It is important to note that these findings are preliminary, tentative, questioning, and based on my own interpretations given the information provided by participants (Creswell, 2003). The intent of this study, as the first of its kind, is to discover the broad range of variables that impact how HSPs experience careers. With a small sample size generalizability cannot be expected, however it should be possible to conduct future research based on identification of significant aspects of participant experiences provided by this study. Further research should be carried out in order to help inform the real world problems HSPs encounter in the workplace and to offer an entry point for understanding and appreciating the 20 percent of our population who are HSPs.

Research Participants

HSPs are approximately 20 percent of the overall population (Aron & Aron, 1997) and belong to every social class, race, gender, and culture. As such this study sought to sample a broad range of individuals from varying backgrounds, since it is the first study of its kind. The 35 participants in this study included 11 males and 24 females. Though I sought equal representation by gender it was difficult to recruit highly sensitive males for this study. Several factors may have played a role. First, the dominant culture in the U.S. espouses a view of the traditional male role as stoic, unemotional, competitive, aggressive, risk-taking, and dominant (Kimmel & Kaufman, 1994). Second, males tend to derive more of their identity from careers than do females and may find discussing career difficulties to be an unpleasant subject. Finally, highly sensitive males may feel conflicted about gender role expectations and be less open to discussing issues that may stimulate further anxiety. Of the highly sensitive males I was able to interview all seemed willing and interested in participation. Only one potential male participant declined to be interviewed, with no reason provided. None of the participants who volunteered for the study were disqualified for unsuitability, though several were unable to participate due to scheduling conflicts.

Participant selection was intended to represent a wide

range of educational backgrounds, but of the 35 participants only three had attained less than a bachelor's degree. Eleven participants hold master's degrees. The lack of representation for participants with less than a bachelor's degree stood in stark contrast to the number holding advanced post-secondary educational credentials. I suggest that participants with less than a bachelor's degree may be less interested in participating because they are more focused on survival and less focused on issues of career fulfillment and may be less inclined to participate because they may not be as familiar with research studies as those who hold advanced degrees. Lastly, this study was announced as one investigating HSPs and careers. It is possible the word "career" may imply I was not interested in those who hold jobs, as opposed to careers, which I define as a series of related positions usually requiring post-secondary education.

Representation of cultures other than the U.S. was important to contrast HSPs' experiences in other countries from those of Americans. One is from Russia, two are from Canada, two are from Denmark, one is from Japan, and one is from China, now living in Canada. The other 28 participants are from different areas of the U.S., with a wide dispersion of states represented.

Seventeen participants are married in heterosexual relationships, one identified as gay and in a relationship, six have never been married, and eleven are either divorced and not remarried or divorced and in a relationship. A wide dispersion of ages was also noted with two from 18-29, 11 from 30-39, 11 from 40-49, 8 from 50-59, 2 from 60-69, and one from 70-79 years old.

A wide variety of careers are represented in this study including education, creative careers in graphic design, writer, fashion design, painting, architecture, musician, interior decorator, television production; helping professions like nursing, yoga instructor , clinical psychologist, social work, and psychodrama therapist; business-related careers in information technology, computer programming, network engineering, software design and development, administrator, self-employed, banking, telecommunications, consulting, sales, airline customer service, actuary, occupational therapy; science careers in electrical and mechanical engineering, laboratory scientist, and horticulture; and finally in the spiritual realm, a minister.

Themes

In order to better understand the multiple realities surrounding HSPs and careers I utilized frequency of mention as well as tacit or felt knowledge (Lincoln & Guba, 1985), to aid me in constructing each theme. In some cases themes were subsumed within other themes or eliminated altogether. I arranged the themes in order of importance for the first three. For the remainder my understanding of the way they interact and influence each other is more akin to a spiral, rather than a linear process. Thus, while the bottom seven themes interact more or less equally the top three seem to exert more influence on the HSPs in this study. The nine themes I arrived at are: empathy, childhood's influence, self-care, rich inner life, creativity, high sensation-seeking, the sociological perspective, work, and the integral being.

These nine themes offer an acknowledgment that individuals do not exist in a vacuum whereby we may understand them strictly in a working context, instead we must examine a complex picture that includes multiple realities. I present each theme with a narrative discussion of each.

Thematic Results

- Theme 1: Empathy
- Theme 2: Childhood's Influence
    - Supportive Childhood
    - Unsupportive Childhood
- Theme 3: Self-Care
    - Protect Self
    - Self-Care Practices
    - Learning to Care for Holistic Self
- Theme 4: Rich Inner Life
    - Sensory
    - Love of Learning
    - Complexity of Thought
- Theme 5: Creativity
    - Curiosity
    - Complexity
    - Need for Creative Engagement
- Theme 6: High Sensation-Seeking
    - Threat of Boredom
    - Curiosity/Exploring
- Theme 7: The Sociological Perspective
    - Experience of High Sensitivity in Other Cultures
    - Effects of Social Class
    - Race

- o Gender
  - ▪ Male Gender Role Conflicts
  - ▪ Male Experience of Androgyny
  - ▪ Embodying Integral Masculinity
- Theme 8: Work
  - o Interpersonal
  - o Physical Environment of Work
  - o Structure of Work
  - o Authentic Work
- Theme 9: The Integral Being
  - o Cultivating Self-Awareness and Radical Self-Acceptance
  - o Learning to Thrive

Theme 1: Empathy

The single biggest factor that all participants in this study mentioned as being predominant in their experience of life is empathy. By empathy I mean the cognitive, affective, and behavioral responses to other people's actual or perceived affective emotional states. The experience of empathy is to some degree universal in humankind, but is especially strong in HSPs (Aron & Aron, 1997; Sangster, 2012) due to their overall greater sensitivity to stimuli. The descriptions I received from participants of empathic sensory stimulation covered a broad range of reaction. Below are some examples of participant reports of empathy,

I notice things about people. I notice their eyes. I can, I know it sounds a little weird and crazy, but I notice aesthetics and I notice things...this guy Gary...one day I was babysitting for Betty and she told me Gary is not allowed to see the boy any more. I found out that he was a pedophile, and I was like so sad. I knew something was wrong with him, but as a child I didn't say anything. All I could do was protect myself. I felt a lot of guilt that I couldn't have saved that little boy from being assaulted that I babysat for. (Taylor)

It is tough enough to be told that you are too sensitive, but I felt overwhelmed, you know, with all the kids and how you know how intense kids are. It was very negative energy for me. I was pretty much a loner from the very beginning in the sense of being around a bunch of people all the time, but when I was probably two years old I could sense people who were kind. It drove my mom nuts, because I would walk up to people in diners and stuff...and I would put my hands up like, hey pick me up, you know, it drove my mom mad. She was afraid I would do that to the wrong person, but I sensed at a very young age who was kind and who wasn't. (Makayla)

I'm like a chameleon, whatever mood somebody around me is in I pick up on it and it...I'm trying to be a little better about it now that I'm aware of it, but I'm very easily influenced by other people's moods and where I'm working now most of us are out at an open pit, there's two, three, four of us in one big open area...so if one of my coworkers is in a bad mood I will definitely pick up on it, and it definitely affects me. (Andrea)

Andrea's account of picking up on the mood of others, or being influenced by it, represents a distinct pattern in this study. HSPs reported that empathy for them means taking in the energy of others, whether they wish to or not. Sometimes this can prove to be an advantage, as for Lily:

> My strengths are in communicating verbally. I can calm anybody down over the phone. I can keep a customer when they are losing a customer. I am very persuasive over the phone and very soothing to people. It is something that has served me well in those jobs. (Lily)

Julia described how empathy helped her better relate to her patients. Instead of seeing them as anonymous "patients" she was able to connect on a more personal level and see them as real people, as she illustrates below:

> I worked as a nurses aid in a nursing home once, and that was probably my most enlightening experiences as having a mature job, where I felt compassion for the residents, you call them residents in nursing homes not patients, and felt like I really actually could make a difference in their lives, as I looked around at the younger and less mature nurses' aides and how they treated the patients and what I could see in the patient and what they couldn't see. You know, that, hey, there really is a person in there and they have dignity and that sort of thing. (Julia)

Dale's work with groups of people in a performance setting requires him to absorb large amounts of emotional energy. He relates his struggle to ascertain problematic expressions from normal expressions:

> I am sensitive to other stuff in the environment too. Just the emotional energy and it really creates challenges for me in working in a theater, because I am always around groups of people and there is always a bunch of emotional energy going on. I will be conducting rehearsal and I would be picking up on little subtle emotional changes in people in the rehearsal and I have to try to filter that out or I have to sort of say, ok this person may look at something and frown and that can be a simple look of concentration not a frown of anger or frustration. (Dale)

Here, Morgan describes how empathy affects her sales responsibilities, with a new element introduced: ethics,

> I was more motivated by knowing the customer and maybe being sensitive to their needs and not wanting to push too far. That seemed to be a struggle for me more than anybody else. You know being sensitive to how or what people are like and we had customers who were like don't try to sell me any single thing and I was very sensitive to that. We have to go out in the aisles and talk to people in the supermarket and I was very sensitive about that. I didn't like people doing that to me in the aisle. I didn't want to do to people what I didn't like done to me. (Morgan)

For Morgan the choice to push customers to buy a product or service is outweighed by the negative energy she would have to take in and process for an extended period of time. This may explain the high number of HSPs who reported having a strong moral compass. The experience of empathy is complex with HSPs noticing negativity and positivity sooner than others. Seth relates that he is "more attuned to people's moods and how various people are doing and just the general feel of the office," but his experience of positive energy has been more limited due to turnover in his office. Seth also reports he enjoys mentoring junior programmers in his office in small groups because he can tell "when someone is just not getting it and try another approach." Hailey explained that her empathy is a major asset in facilitating connection with others in her work as a nurse, in her words:

> They liked me, they liked to talk to me, and open up to me. I have some gift that people like to open up to me. If I can be calm and listen they like to talk to me and they still do. People confide in me in things.

Hailey's sense of empathy enables her to notice subtle physical distinctions in patients others miss:

> If they're hurting I can hear, if they're hot in their breathing I can tell because I am so sensitive to them. I can see in their faces if they look like they're in distress. They can be happy too! Umm...I have monitors too and I can tell any fluctuations because I'm keen to noticing changes.

Finally, Lucy related how her empathy carried over to scholarly pursuits:

> I still don't like math or history in the way it was taught with dates and people's names and things like that. I was more about what was happening to the people at the time.

One of the distinguishing features of SPS is cognitive depth of processing or the extent to which stimuli are processed in the brain. In HSPs this depth of processing is deeper than in others. HSPs report that their sense of empathy exposes them to stimulation they largely find themselves unable to turn off, thus they tend to dwell or ruminate on events that occur on and off the job.

Theme 2: Childhood's Influence

The theme of childhood influences emerged as one of the most significant in my data analysis. The review of the literature explicated the primary distinction among HSPs has to do with the experience of support or non-support in childhood (Aron & Aron, 1997). By support I refer to nurturing, love, and parental response to needs expressed when we are very young. The underlying mechanism for this distinction seems to be the depth of processing that occurs in the brains of HSPs, thus for those who experience unsupportive parenting the negativity is processed to a far greater degree, with resultant effects throughout the life course (Gunnar, 1994; Weissbluth, 1989; Aron et al, 2005; Aron, 2006; Aron et al., 2012), similarly for those who experience supportive parenting; they tend to do much better because the positivity is processed more deeply. I began my interviews by asking about the participant's background. Some participants clearly stated that they had experienced neglect, abuse, instability, and even chaos in the home.

Unsupportive childhoods.

The following quotes present a view of unsupportive childhoods:

I could never please my father. He was verbally and physically abusive to me, maybe because I was the first born, I don't know. I am not sure, it always felt like there were expectations. (Joshua)

They wanted all of us to be well behaved, not talk back, do what they say. If you refused to do what they say, they got very angry at you. They would remind you all the time that you did this terrible thing whatever it was. (Kent)

I didn't go to school very much, my mother was a very sick person...um...and that's who ended up in the 70s getting custody of us. It didn't matter then, men didn't get custody of their kids. So, as sick as she was I ended up with her and being the oldest I was expected to stay home and help care for these kids while she was, you know, involved in whatever people like her do, usually its bad things. (Hailey)

I was always fractured...My adoptive parents had great issues. They were uneducated and simple people. What we might call unenlightened people having their own struggles and issues in life. My entrance in their life was more problematic than it was a blessing apparently. I was mostly neglected for the most part they were not supportive and loving. Basically, I was just there invisible with little spurts of affection. (Julia)

My parents were actively neglectful. They were actively parenting for the most part, but they were so wrapped up in themselves. My dad was pretty much work, he had a 1955 attitude. I will take care of the family when I am home and I can do what I want to for myself. He was constantly, both of my parents had nonstop contact. You just could not overact for anything. (Lily)

Participants expressed a variety of ways parents neglected their needs, either consciously or unconsciously. Parental acceptance of SPS also came into question and I asked some participants if their parents accepted their sensitivity. Results indicate parents of males tended to be less accepting, even hostile to males expressing sensitivity. Kirk relates his emerging understanding of his father's view of sensitivity and a perception that Kirk needed to hide his sensitivity:

I had the perception that everybody was like me, especially as a boy as I started working through the grades in school. It became more obvious through experience that sensitivity was something that I needed to keep to myself. It was basically a punishable offense, not in school, but with my dad. He was not respectful of that trait in me at all. I began to understand that it was unusual and I began to understand that it was not acceptable both in terms of how I got along with the other boys and girls to a certain point.

This lack of acceptance may breed deep feelings of inadequacy, low self-esteem, and a pessimistic explanatory style (Seligman, 2006). Explanatory style becomes the lens through which we view everyday happenings. For those who view each event as permanent, pervasive, and personal the world becomes a very defeating place. HSPs are particularly susceptible to negativity, which can lead to more depression, anxiety, lower overall satisfaction in life, and general poor health.

Supportive childhoods.

Contrasting the negative stimulation accompanying an unsupportive childhood are the following examples of supportive childhoods reported by participants:

We had a very quiet middle class. We didn't have trauma. We didn't have anything like a lot of the kids I saw. My parents were still together after 52 years. (Lucy)

They have completely dedicated their lives to me and

my brother and they pretty much let me join any activity that I wanted to. I took archery and all different kinds of outdoor activities when I was a kid. They embraced me for being different. Mom and dad when I got home, they liked being a safe haven. They were very loving, very supportive. (Makayla)

I believe I'm blessed with my father because he's a philosophy teacher, religion professor so he kind of, kind of exposed us to many different opinions and cultures and religions which I believe are a blessing. (Aubree)

I think because my parents put their internal operations before anything else they were always incredibly supportive of both my brother and I. (Olivia)

I noted that participants who reported supportive childhoods in general seemed to have derived a protective effect from parental support and seemed to feel freer to try new things without anxiety or fear. Similarly, I noted that those HSPs whose parents emphasized a spiritual practice seemed to do much better than those who did not. Olivia expressed her spiritually-centered upbringing as the "biggest influence in my life." I cover this in more depth later in theme nine.

The delineation between what constitutes a good or bad childhood, in cases where the participant did not provide information denoting instability, neglect, abuse, or chaos, is where my judgment as a researcher is privileged. In those cases I surmised from a combination of statements referring to negative interactions with others that a participant experienced an unsupportive childhood. Again, it is the depth of processing of negativity or positivity that seems to matter with regard to impact on later life experiences. Thus, one may experience supportive parenting as a child, yet experience trauma in school, in social interactions, or develop a pessimistic explanatory style that effectively outweighs the positive aspects in the home (Seligman, 2006). The threshold I used for considering a childhood as supportive is marginal. Aron and Aron (1997) suggested that "any situation that is marginally problematic for the average child could be more disturbing for the highly sensitive child" (p. 355). Thus, one did not need to have a perfect, trauma-free childhood to be considered as having a supportive childhood.

Of the 35 participants in the study 19 were determined to have likely experienced supportive childhoods, while 16 were determined to have likely experienced unsupportive childhoods. Furthermore, among the small group of high sensation seekers five experienced unsupportive childhoods and three experienced supportive childhoods. The number of participants is almost evenly split and represents a greater number than the one third Aron and Aron (1997) reported. This near equity may suggest the percentage of unsupportive childhoods may be greater than originally determined.

Theme 3: Self-Care

Throughout the course of conducting this study the

theme of self-care emerged consistently. By self-care I am referring to the practices and habits that HSPs engage in to find or maintain a sense of overall health and well-being. As elucidated in the two previous themes HSPs begin life on one of two possible tracts, either a supportive or unsupportive one. For both groups the experience of empathy necessitates that they develop ways of shielding themselves from negative or overstimulation. HSPs do this in a variety of ways. One way is through developing a life orientation directed primarily at protecting themselves, avoiding risks, preferring the familiar, and engaging in self-care practices that produce the effect of calm and balance. In this theme I present three major areas that participants in the study described as important to them: protection of self, specific self-care practices, and learning to care for holistic self. By holistic self I mean emotional, physical, and spiritual aspects of oneself.

Protect self.

The first area that emerged in this theme is a strongly expressed need to protect oneself from negative stimulation. Negative stimulation can come in many forms in the workplace, including sensory stimuli like bright lights, strong smells, uncomfortable temperatures, and poorly designed work spaces. Negative stimulation can also be of an interpersonal nature with HSPs primarily reporting a dislike for competitive, aggressive individuals, but also for environments that force socialization or contain conflict. All 35 participants articulated a strong need to shield themselves from negative stimulation, with those from unsupportive childhoods expressing it most strongly. Hailey describes how she tried adapting in her nursing career,

> I requested a specific hall, because I knew that hall
> was a lighter hall, an easier hall of people to deal with.
> These residents didn't require quite as much help,
> they weren't as bad as some of the other halls and that
> protected me from some of the overstimulation.

The need to protect oneself seems to take many forms,
from avoiding overstimulation due to workload, as for Hailey
in the above quote, to Kurt's need to separate himself from
an early, chaotic home environment,

> Basically I think I, because of all the chaos and trauma
> and things that were going on in my home, I think I
> just shut down and I didn't really know what I
> wanted. Myself I couldn't focus on anything other
> than what was happening around me, so my outlook
> was basically sports, so I ended up playing football
> and leaving and just not being in the house most of
> the time. I found that I organized my life in a way that
> I can stay away from the chaos.

Others articulated the way on-the-job stresses affected their
functioning, as for Joshua as he describes his work as a
psychodrama therapist,

> Clinical psychodrama bored me. It finally burned me
> out. We are the ones that deal with a lot of people in
> these groups and you are taking on all their energy.
> You really have to work hard to protect yourself,
> because you will absorb a lot of poison. You are
> dealing with people who are victims of sexual abuse,

physical abuse and trauma, and just a whole manner of issues. It just eventually I felt like I had been a combat veteran and I had just seen too much... was I stopped getting into supervision and supervision was not about how you practice, but who you are as a practitioner. I really was not taking care of myself. It was hard dealing with what I was dealing with. You can only deal with so much trauma on a daily basis before it just gets to you. I didn't have anywhere to process that. I think that was the ultimate end of it for me.

Some participants intuitively realized the need to protect oneself early in life, as Taylor articulated,

It was hard, like being so sensitive and knowing thing and people were not always so safe. I feel it was this intuition in myself that kept me safe and my sister and I used to play this game where we would imagine this over healing light. It always started like a solar plexus and then we would emanate it. I remember that would become a meditation habit for me and it made me feel very safe and warm. I would extend it out to my family, almost like a prayer meditation. I feel like it kept my father safe on the water, it kept my brother safe, it kept my sisters safe, and all this kind of stuff. It was just like a game that we played. It was funny because in the last couple of years I have actually been doing some work with shamans. This is a technique that they used. I think it is amazing that my sister as a child intuitively knew this technique. I believe everything is energy and we manifest reality with our thoughts. I think that when you do that, it is not only comforting to you like a blanket or a teddy bear, but it is empowering. I also think it is effective.

Seventy percent of HSPs are introverted (Aron & Aron, 1997) or prefer to focus on their interior processes. Samantha relates her experience early in life,

> I learned very young to literally shut out everything around me and just go to a book. That was pretty much how I spent every moment, almost like I was being forced to interact with people, because it was my only real escape, my only relief from it. I knew that everybody else didn't feel like that, so of course as a small child I felt very like there was something wrong with me...I knew I was different and I thought I was just a bad person so I just crawled into myself for a very long time. I didn't have a lot of friends. I didn't really go places. I didn't really do stuff. It wasn't until college that I started to find my way to geekdom.

I was interested in how deep introversion affects career choice so I prompted Samantha to explain that a little more. She replied:

> I have a very primal motivation that I don't want other people to have the childhood I had. I don't want people to have the life I have had. That underlies an enormous amount of what I do. I was treated in very unfortunate and unpleasant ways and I will be damned if I will let that happen to anybody else. There

is a huge protective streak. There is a huge sense of wanting to make life better and there is a huge sense that each of us has something of importance. I spent a lot of time being told that I was over sensitive, and that I was immature, and that I was this and I was that. To look back on all of that and say all of these things have created a person who generally speaking is pretty damn empathic and is able to walk in other people's shoes and help other people out and let other people see another perspective. That is playing to the world that I have created. My whole motivation is that I don't want other people to live the life I have had to. I want them to have a better shot. I sort of fight for at least my little corner to be a nicer place. (Samantha)

Samantha's experience turned into a spiritual mission to protect others. Other HSPs related similar external orientations even if they began life focused inwardly. Regardless of when HSPs realize the need to protect themselves, they consider self-protection a priority. As Faith expressed "you cannot expose your vulnerabilities too much, because this world will eat you alive." As Evelyn continues,

It's hard for HSP's in the work environment...it is still very difficult for me to put up that wall, to shield myself from all those feelings out there and not be affected by other people's feelings. We are labelled as different and sometimes targeted. I mean my last job my manager definitely tormented me. I was the scapegoat. If anything went wrong, it was my fault, which was ludacris. (Evelyn)

Evelyn differentiated empathy as physical, emotional, or spiritual, with herself falling into the emotional category. She later revealed that she "already had a tendency towards picking up on nonverbal signals. I had a mother where it helped being able to step into the room and have a feeling or an idea what the vibes were." In that sense it seems HSPs learn how to utilize empathy in a very pragmatic manner.

HSPs reported feeling they needed to protect themselves whether they were from unsupportive or supportive backgrounds. Congruent with that overarching need is specific self-care practices.

Self-care practices.

A self-care practice is intended to mean any activity engaged in that facilitates a sense of calmness, centeredness, balance, and health, emotionally, physically, and spiritually. A variety of practices emerged from the coding process including meditation, yoga, connection to nature, motorcycle riding, attention to diet and exercise, setting boundaries, and purposeful selection of friends. These all seemed to be of great importance to participants. Some participants placed a higher value on self-care than they did on career advancement expressing that their emotional, physical, and spiritual lives have to be in order before they can take on additional demands.

Vitaly explains the value of caring for himself as most important in his life,

Personal growth is something very important to me. It

is actually more important than my career at this point...my personal growth is more important to me so I think career growth is a violation of myself, that is why I am not into consider career growth as my number one priority. (Vitaly)

He relates his routine for self-care involves physical exercise "I have a routine of four days per week that I do these exercises at whatever the costs. I started like this routine the last month and a half."

Yoga was reported as a major outlet for self-care by participants. Yoga has been practiced for thousands of years and is primarily intended as a means of attaining a continuous state of peace of mind so one might truly experience oneself and unite with the universal. In Western countries Hatha yoga is primarily practiced for its physical benefits, but also for its inherent spirituality. The approach varies by practitioner with some participants reporting deeper involvement, while others focus on the physical aspects. Lucy began practicing yoga by taking classes, soon realizing yoga was her "heart opener." She found yoga allowed her to focus inwardly and "stop being what everybody wanted me to be" (Lucy). Lucy eventually began teaching yoga classes and developed a small business helping others find their true selves. Molly also began practicing yoga, in her words "I started practicing yoga as a way to cope with my features and my panic attacks. I started doing that when I was about eighteen or nineteen and it helps tremendously" (Molly).

Other participants related that self-care for them

means learning to be completely self-aware. Kent, for instance, has learned to be more aware of the specific sources of overstimulation and be more flexible in order to avoid them. He is especially triggered by grocery stores, as are many other participants, and if he feels overwhelmed he simply comes back at another time when it is less crowded. Kent seems to be attuned to his internal states and is able to manage them based on this awareness. Bruce has also learned to manage his emotional life by what he describes as "post processing" with another person, rather than "taking in those feelings on his own." Adelle has developed a more active approach that includes swimming, walking, reading and talking with others. She describes self-humor or being able to laugh at oneself as a way of minimizing stressful events as helpful. Adelle emphasized the role of "sharing our gifts with others" as crucial for her.

Olivia incorporates Zumba dance in her set of self-care practices and describes its value in her life:

> I do a lot of yoga, I have a meditation practice, now I have a writing practice every day. Interestingly, lately in terms of taking care of my body, I have started taking Zumba dance classes, which usually might not have been something I picked, because I was spending so much time writing and thinking and reading. There is something exciting about being playful and dancing to music. It is one of those circumstances when you are not actually interacting with others like in a group and not having to have a fun time, but I think that was always reviving to me when I see these parts of myself that...there is intentionally a contradiction who wants

something more to engage with or the part of me that wants to be quiet and sometimes they can even in a given day be in a different place.

Olivia also related to me how she carefully manages her energies "if I am really able to manage my day and my week, then my colleagues never see the part of me that hits the limits." Olivia's responses suggested that setting boundaries is important to HSPs. Boundaries may be limitations one sets that prevents overstimulation or negative stimulation. Joshua's approach is to carefully choose who he spends his time with, thus regulating the stimuli he takes in. He is, however, not an isolationist, rather he has found that as he gets older his patience for having to deal with negative stimulation is less. This lessening of patience as one ages for negative or overstimulation was a nearly universal sentiment expressed by participants in this study. Setting boundaries, in that sense, becomes not only a matter of choosing whom to connect with, but also a matter of self-preservation.

In addition to the practices outlined above HSPs expressed a fundamental need to reappraise how they care for themselves, how they perceive life, and how they should live. This orientation was not in place at a young age for the majority of HSPs in this study. Rather they seem to have learned the necessity of self-care after years of career and life stress.

Learning to care for holistic self.

The sense of learning a new way of caring for oneself

emerged out of the coding process and integrated the two previous aspects of protecting oneself and developing self-care practices. I began to get a sense that the HSPs I spoke with were aware of the need to care for body, mind, and spirit and valued it deeply. HSPs in this study described caring for the body through diet and exercise, appropriate periods of rest and recuperation, and through developing a greater awareness of somatic symptoms of overstimulation. Caring for the mind takes the form of reading, writing, creative engagement, and connecting deeply with others. Finally, participants expressed a desire/need to connect with the divine or universal through meditation and other contemplative activities that remove the focus from the ego and encourages authentic awareness in the present moment. Joshua expressed, for example, that he is motivated by "being completely in my body and sensitized to where I am 100 percent present" as most important. Participants in this study ranked their connection to nature as one that facilitated and supported connection to the divine or universal.

Theme 4: Rich Inner Life

I realized early in designing this study that it was necessary to explore the inner lives of participants to the extent this is possible in qualitative research to acquire any real understanding of how they experience careers. By inner life I refer to the inner psychic processes such as contemplation, reflection, introspection, sensory, and intellect. In this theme I present an accounting of participant responses related to sensory experience, the love of learning and sense of curiosity many expressed and, finally, complexity of thought.

Sensory.

The sensory experiences of HSPs are perhaps the most common way the public at large understands SPS. By sensory I mean the stimulation taken in by our senses of hearing, smell, vision, touch, and taste. Participants in this study reported sensitivities to a wide variety of stimuli. Many participants reported feeling "overwhelmed" or distracted by stimuli that might not affect other people as deeply. Below are quotes from participants detailing the kinds of sensory stimuli that cause them to feel overwhelmed or to which they feel particularly sensitive,

> It was too bright. It was too cold. It was too hot. Everything was just too much. It took years and years for that to even remotely settle down... my house was very loud and chaotic and noisy. We had dogs and cats and this and that and all I wanted to do was to crawl into a book. I learned very young to literally shut out everything around me...I remember when I went to college, it was horrible, and I went to a small school. I was in a classroom with like thirty people and it was just like overwhelming. It was terrible and loud and noisy. They rattled their desks and scooted their chairs. It was just awful. I did not think I was going to make it in college at all. (Samantha)

> It was the constant stimulation, the people running around in back of me doing things...the first time

anybody ever said anything to me about looking anxious was when I couldn't find the button I needed to push to order their meal and I was shaking and that person told me "it's ok, calm down." And I didn't even realize it, they saw it, but I didn't know I was doing it, so I guess to them I was overanxious, but I was very overstimulated...I felt so tired and so overwhelmed...it was it was just call lights going off, sounds overhead, griping at each other, patients crying out in pain. I had a lady who was a double amputee in a lot of pain. (Hailey)

The stimulation that comes into a nurse's daily life in a hospital is you just wouldn't believe, you cannot imagine it, for instance, you are standing there at the nurse's server, that is the door outside the patient's room, you are carrying a Netcom phone, which hourly beeps to give you instructions to do something that you can't and you are not wanting to do anyway, but they decided that you need to be reminded anyway so the phone goes off. The phone is ringing and the patients family comes out and talks to you and there is a big sweeper or shampooer shampooing the rug all the way up and down several times behind your back and there is announcements over head at the same time then the fire alarm drill goes off, ding, ding, ding, ding. I mean it is just sometimes, I just have to stand there plant my feet and stare and just take it moment by moment until it goes away if I cannot get out of it at the moment...the stimulation as a hospital nurse is immense. (Julia)

If there was just kind of a constant really busy day, so constantly dealing with people and, say, that goes on for a period of three hours. I am so frazzled when I am done, that I kind of have to just completely zone out and not talk to anyone for an extended period of time. (Molly)

I cannot stand loud talking. If I am on this train and hear loud talking, I literally get out and go to another train. It just drives me nuts how loud people are talking. I can't take it when I am on a train. When I am on a bus, I can tolerate it, you know, if I ask them to quiet down they give me a hard time about it. Chewing, I can't stand chewing. People who chew with their mouth open just bugs me. It sounds like smacking, you know, chomp, chomp, chomp. There is a guy at work now that does it and I say, "uhh hum" and I actually wrote down how many times a day he did it. I asked him about it and he said it was a new thing, it went on for a month, but he has quieted down so everything is ok, but he was driving me nuts. I go around asking people around him if they hear him and they say yeah, so no one speaks out...when people are eating chips out of the bag and it crinkles, they eat one chip at a time and they go back in the bag and it sounds like, you know, it jars my ears. It just irritates the hell out of me. I just usually walk away and take a walk or something. (Kent)

It is important to note that HSPs do not possess extra-sensitive senses, rather it is the depth to which stimuli are processed in the brain. Thus, to a HSP strong smells, bright overhead lights, noises, and tense social situations may be overwhelming or distracting to an uncomfortable degree. HSPs in this study reported sensitivities to the above-described stimuli, but not all HSPs are distracted or feel overwhelmed by the same things. Some HSPs reported experiencing problems with bright lights, while others reported a need for bright light. Similarly, some HSPs have less sensitivity to one or more of the above described stimuli. The HSPs in this study reflect a non-homogenous group with individual tolerances determined by probable random variation, but is likely influenced by individual efforts at desensitization to certain sensory stimuli due to cultural pressures to conform.

The sensory life of HSPs is complex with overstimulation representing a common issue. However, HSPs in this study report a greater capacity for enjoyment of stimulation when they are able to control the type and duration. Participants mentioned a deep enjoyment of music, an appreciation for the fine and performing arts, and general heightened aesthetics in all aspects of life.

Love of learning.

HSPs, due to their ability to notice subtle differences before others are predisposed to taking in a wealth of stimuli (Aron & Aron, 1997). While this may be problematic for many HSPs in terms of overstimulation the capacity for learning seems to be large. Participants in this study reported a deep love of learning. Below are some examples from participants:

> I like taking pictures a lot. I was always into writing. That was always kind of my thing. I was into reading and writing and I still am...I think I always wanted to be a writer. I gradually wanted to become a teacher as well, my whole family is kind of a family of teachers. (Colleen)

> I am not only sitting in my house and I go on trips and I am very curious. I try to find the meaning about things and I read a lot and I study a lot...I don't think my curiosity will stop. I read about things and I am so curious... In childhood I always had to be something had to study. (Astrid)

> I wrote a play. I acted it out. I wrote it. I role played about me. I did that last year. I never wrote a play in my life. I took writing classes, play writing classes at a place in town. I took photography. I have taken dancing. I was in taekwondo for a while. (Kent)

> I think that ah...think that the internet and ability to do online classes is just the greatest thing ever for me. I love it! I am so happy that I do have so much to do now...I've always been incredibly curious about everything. (Ava)

Participants reported having a wide variety of

interests that do not seem to diminish with age. I was curious about how this love of learning applied to careers and asked participants if it is important to them that they have potential for growth and development within their chosen career. I expected most to answer in the affirmative, but was surprised by the depth to which participants placed great value on the need to be afforded opportunities to learn new skills and be able to grow intellectually in a position. Several participants provided contrasting responses, however and emphasized that learning new things often meant uncertainty about expectations, which stimulated anxiety. Those participants were all from unsupportive backgrounds.

Complexity of thought.

SPS works through a natural complexity of thought as the agent through which stimulation is processed in the brains of HSPs. Along with a love of learning participants reported that they have a natural liking for complex thinking and a strong dislike for superficiality. Olivia describes her propensities here:

> I realized that I am very contemplative. I like a lot of my work to be big picture. I like to be reflecting on things. I am not a big doer, I mean, I am not the person who can set up big meetings and stuff like, let's get packing or like, let's not sit around and talk about ideas, let's get to work... I realize that I am much more comfortable in the world of ideas when I am in the world. In the world of action I have no reflection whatsoever. If I have to pick one or the other, I want

to be in the world of contemplation, thinking, and ideas.

The emphasis on "big picture" thinking was offset by other reports of liking highly detailed work, such as Seth, "I was a tinkerer. I loved to take things apart and see how they worked and figure things out and building things. I was always really good with math and science." The majority of HSPs in this study reported a strong dislike for math, while a minority reported a strong liking for math and science. Seth's description of desiring to understand the interrelationships between components inside electrical devices echoed the theme of complexity of thought, albeit in a more focused manner. Evelyn related how complexity of thought can also be an unwanted asset in a work situation:

> It's the old canary in the coal mine phenomenon where there is dysfunction in a work situation, somehow I would get involved, either, it will be directed at me and I was intelligent enough to see what was going on and the dysfunction under the surface. Unfortunately, most of the places I have worked they really are interested in that. It can be useful information, you know, like the canary in the coal mine or it can be the fact we don't want to deal with the fact that we could be contributing or causing the problem.

The "canary in the coal mine" phrase was used repetitively by many participants in this study to describe how they often feel while at work. Being naturally predisposed toward big picture, long-term thinking privileges one with knowing what may happen if a given course is taken or not altered. Participants, however, did not report that this ability was valued by employers or understood, as in the aforementioned quote.

With this ability to think in complex terms a number of participants reported giftedness in school or graduating from college with high honors. In Linda's case her giftedness translated into academic achievement with a bachelor's degree in mechanical engineering, a master's in nutrition and a master's in divinity. In other cases recognition of early giftedness did not necessarily translate to career success in terms of a linear trajectory of increasingly responsible and rewarding positions. Instead, in the cases of Faith and Lucy, their natural complexity of thought seems to have entailed a longer journey of self-discovery, as Faith relates:

> I had never ever to this day I have never known what I wanted to do when I grow up. I still don't know...I was so confused that my folks actually sent me to a psychologist that was working with the people out at my dad's place and they had me do some vocational testing...I really felt underutilized all of my life.

Lucy's work experiences eventually led her to self-employment where she was able to blend together her interests in teaching yoga, consulting with other HSPs to help them find their authentic selves, and living in a manner that acknowledges complexity. This complexity of thought is a key component that influences the way HSPs in this study experience their careers.

Theme 5: Creativity

One of the most frequently mentioned words by participants in this study was creativity. HSPs, by virtue of their ability to notice subtleties before others, greater capacity for aesthetic enjoyment, complexity of mind, and sense of curiosity are innately predisposed toward creativity (Aron & Aron, 1997). In this study approximately 75 percent of participants described themselves as "creative." By creative I imply a broader definition than commonly expressed. Barron (1995) defined creativity as "the ability to respond adaptively to the need for new ways of being...the ability to bring something new into existence" (p. 31). Barron elucidated a common core of characteristics that appear consistently across fields: independence of judgment; a preference for complexity; a strong desire to create; a deep motivation or drive--which Barron called the cosmological motive--to create one's own universe of meaning, personally defined; lots of personal troubles linked to an intense sensibility; a strongly intuitive nature; and patience or endurance, persistence, and basic optimism in the face of difficulty.

Pairing Barron's (1995) encapsulation with Csikszentmihalyi's (1996) contention that "the one word that makes creative people different is *complexity*" (p. 57) referring to an ability to express "the full range of traits that are potentially present in the human repertoire" (p. 57) and Storr's (1993) view that the "one feature of creative people is their capacity for change and development...linked to their openness to their own feelings and emotions and also to impressions and new ideas from outside" (p. 301) I determined, utilizing the aforementioned definition, that over 90 percent of participants were likely creative. Of the remaining 10 percent it is likely their issues with anxiety, fear, and depression inhibit any significant development of creativity. In this theme I present a view of creativity as expressed by participants.

Curiosity.

Creativity, as defined by Barron, (1995) is a four-stage process. The first stage is preparation with curiosity as a necessary first component of the creative act. A strong sense of curiosity was evident in the data analysis process that seemed to encompass subjective and objective foci. Some participants related a curiosity to acquire knowledge that has breadth and depth, such as Lucy "My husband just left, he said I need a computer with the ability to have ten browsers open at one time, because I am always researching and reading at the same time. I want to learn something more about what I just read." Ava explained that her sense of creativity is a path where variety and acquisition of new knowledge is important to her for personal growth and development, but the basis behind it is curiosity about "everything in life." This fundamental sense of curiosity was common among participants and I was interested how this works within a career context. Linda related to me how her experiences:

> I tend to think of ideas as being sticky. If something happens at work or if something happens in my studies or I just have some other brain storms about theology I usually can't let it go for quite a few hours,

maybe even two days. Sometimes it is very valuable because I can take the idea farther and it takes a while to take it farther in a different direction than it is going to turn out pretty cool once I am writing about it. I know that other people wouldn't do that. They wouldn't spend the time on it.

Participants primarily related that it is important for them to do work that allows them to indulge their curiosity and variety of interests. Boredom and the threat of boredom was often cited as significant factors in leaving a position or feeling unsatisfied in a position.

Complexity.

The topic of complexity of thought has been previously been elucidated as part of the rich inner lives of HSPs, but complexity here means an openness to new experiences internally and externally and a manifestation of a broad range of human expressions and traits simultaneously. Of the HSPs in this study who identified as creative individuals a complexity of mind was evident along with an openness to new experience. Some expressed their participation in the study was driven by their desire to participate in the unfolding complexity of new research directly addressing issues they feel very passionately about.

Few participants desired or exemplified simplicity of trait expression, instead relating a "big picture" of their lives steeped in complexity and nuance. Participants described their openness to new experience as central to their experience of life. Of the few who described less openness their primary motivation seemed to be fear and anxiety about change.

Creative engagement.

Participants in this study expressed a need for creative engagement on many levels. Linda related "I also had some interest in architecture and just drawing. I am a visual thinker and a systems thinker, so things related to that. I also like dealing with materials, so dealing with materials or other things that you can get your hands into." Linda's preference is for a working environment where her creativity is "encouraged and utilized." Claire emphasized that creative engagement for her means more than simply being viewed as a "design monkey." In her view creative engagement is about the freedom and autonomy to engage her curiosity in meaningful ways that honors and builds on all of her skills and abilities that matters,

> I like the type of graphic design where I could combine my painting with graphic design, so a lot of the books that I made I used original paintings to scan them in and use them as part of the book. That was a really great experience. I had that full control over what I was designing and all the content and was able to research what I wanted to do. That was great. (Claire)

The need for a certain degree of creative control seemed to be important to many participants. Autonomy of action was another major element participants valued. Though most participants stated that they liked to work in quiet environment at times, or alone, they also articulated a need to collaborate in small groups. Finally, several participants described a token desire for creativity on the part of organizations or companies they had worked for. Linda related how in several of her positions, as she was close to leaving each position, her supervisor would tell her they "wanted creativity, but not that much." This organizational fear of creativity belies the need to remain abreast of competitive pressures, which I will examine more fully in my discussion of theme five in the next chapter.

Theme 6: High Sensation-Seeking

A small percentage of HSPs also possess a trait known as high sensation-seeking (Zuckerman, 1979, 1983, 1991, 2007, 2009). High sensation seeking [HSS] can be divided into four separate traits, adventure or thrill-seeking, experience seeking, disinhibition, and boredom susceptibility. I was aware of this trait prior to conducting the study and personally identified as a HSS/HSP, but did not specifically expect to encounter other HSS/HSPs in this study since the percentage is thought to be small. Of the 35 participants in this study eight identified as HSS/HSPs. My impressions is several more are likely high sensation seekers, but have not examined this likelihood because some are still relatively new to identifying as HSPs. There are noticeable differences in HSPs who are also high sensation seekers. Below I provide an accounting of the most prominent distinctions as I view them at present.

Threat of boredom.

Boredom and the threat of boredom were mentioned most often by participants who are HSS/HSPs in this study. Taylor described her experiences as follows:

> Boredom is my worst enemy. I would, there is no way, if there was a job that I do that is boring I quit. I was working at a grocery store and lasted three hours. They wanted me to bag groceries over and over and over again until I got it right. I was like I got it right the second time, because I go to the grocery store and I bag my groceries anyways. I have had these jobs where I am like if I am bored I just go to them and say, I am so sorry, sometimes I would say I was offered another job, but if it is like boredom I can't do it. I don't know what I would do if I was bored. I can't do the same thing, it is my worst enemy.

Taylor and Adelle are extraverts in addition to being HSS/HSPs. Adelle related, "the constraint of the work and the boredom because it was boring and there was nothing exciting to do, I was restless." This sense of restlessness for HSS/HSPs may be so profound that they may feel the only way they can escape from it is to quit the job and attempt to find another one that satisfies their needs. I specifically noted in my data analysis that the HSS/HSPs in this study were also the most highly creative individuals and several-- Taylor and Adelle--specifically self-identified as highly creative. Boredom and the threat of boredom due to repetitious tasks or being around "boring" individuals is a significant aspect of the way HSS/HSP's experience their careers.

Curiosity/exploring.

Contrary to the popular notion of high sensation-seeking as exclusively thrill-seeking, participants in this study described high sensation-seeking primarily in terms of curiosity and a need to explore in furtherance of their personal growth and development. Thus, it is experience seeking in sensory and intellectual domains that seems to be most important to participants. Bruce stated "I was just kind of seeking adventure and growing up outside and trying to find new places to go. I explored the neighborhood a lot on my bike and just was always looking for adventure." Concurrent with boredom is the need to seek new stimulation. Often this means HSS/HSPs must arrange their working lives in unconventional ways to accommodate their need for new and novel stimulation. Chouko described her experiences:

> I am high sensation-seeking, but I cannot stay too long in one place that is why I didn't get a full-time job. I have to move around. One job is not enough...Yes, different, like teaching, psychotherapy, and housewife. I teach, I help my husband's job...he is a lot of things to me or I get bored...people tell me to concentrate on researcher, but I can't. I cannot do this as a full-time though, because I get bored... so I want to do something I can finish. I like making things. I make bags and stuff. I mean sewing too...I want to try something new if it looks very interesting, but at the same time I need to withdraw it. I need time...Always,

I am fighting with it.

Chouko's description of high sensation-seeking as continuously pushing forward in search of new experiences is common among participants in this study. The highly sensitive side is more reserved and prefers to observe, contemplate, and engage in limited or controlled thrills. Chouko also related how she prefers to work on projects of short duration to avoid the likelihood of boredom. Bruce's preference for projects is similar. He articulated the value of being a high sensation-seeker thusly,

> It's very interesting. Every day is different. I think that is what it comes down to for me, is that I am a lot of it is that I really listen to myself and say what kind of energy do I have today. Some days I have a lot of energy and can do a lot, but other days if I have been through a stressful situation the day before I need to do self-care, so the balance is really tricky, but I appreciate the framework now...because I was all over the place you know, but now I feel like I have been able to find a balance. I do appreciate that it does being high sensation-seeker, it does give me the motivation to be creative and to kind of work through things when I need it. There is an advantage to it. (Bruce)

Bruce also denoted a need to balance his sensation-seeking side with his highly sensitive side,

> I find that I am the most balanced than I have been earlier in my life. I think my high sensation kind of

dominated more because that is how I got acceptance from other people, but now I am really embracing my sensitive side, so I find that is kind of more at my age that is what is coming out.

Joshua's experience was different. He worked as a psychodrama therapist only finding a need for balance after completely burning himself out. He stated:

It was a high action a lot of activity. Everything is about spontaneity and creativity and those are two traits that I wanted to develop in myself. Even as I was directing, was developing that because in directing you have to be spontaneous and very creative in the moment and all the time under pressure. I like that. It is kind of like running down the street with your hair on fire. It was just, it made me feel powerful....I couldn't handle doing what people wanted me to do...what I do realize is I was burning out the whole time...I was getting stressed, pretty stressed and I was working hard and I started feeling that. I was doing groups in psychiatric hospitals and it was becoming uncreative to me. It was just doing the same things over and over again. I got tired of it and bored. I wanted to get into a more creative aspect of psychodrama and then the mechanical aspect of it, and so I think, see clinical psychodrama bored me...It finally burned me out. (Joshua)

For those who are HSS/HSPs the need for self-care

becomes even more crucial, as does possessing a high degree of self-knowledge or self-awareness. The potential benefits of being highly creative and driven to seek out novelty and new stimulation may require substantial efforts to know oneself.

Theme 7: The Sociological Perspective

The impact of the broader social contexts in which we live was expected to exert significant influence on the lived experiences of participants. By broad social context I mean social location or the society participants are a part of and influenced by. Each society has its own specific characteristics within which individuals live and act. C. Wright Mills (1959) explained that "the sociological perspective enables us to grasp the connection between history and biography" (p. 71-72). By history Mills was referring to the collection of specific events that form and shape a society's ideas about various aspects of life like beliefs, rules, and roles. By biography Mills meant our specific experiences within the society that produce an orientation toward life. Our location in society largely determines what we do and how we think. This theme encompasses several major social components that determine how participants experience life including culture, social class, race, and gender.

Culture.

This study was designed primarily to better understand the lived experiences of HSPs in the U.S., but I felt it would be generative to have a small representative sample from other countries included in the study. Five countries, besides the U.S., are represented in this study including Russia, Denmark, Japan, Canada, and China. In this section I will provide an accounting of the major points covered by participants with results for each country.

Vitaly, the participant from Russia, related that in his experience HSPs in Russia are not accepted or understood. His experience of childhood included clashes with traditional gender role expectations from his step-father who subscribed to a traditional male ideal of physical punishment. Vitaly recounted that his memories of that time in his life are centered on his step-father's use of physical punishment, which evoked the "strongest emotions" from that period of his life. Vitaly's work in customer service places certain demands on him to adapt to environmental and interpersonal working conditions. He expressed, with regards to HSPs:

> This job that I am doing right now. It is not very my thing 100 percent and I am sure my employer would agree with me and would find a replacement, but they are not for now which is good. Again, a job does not babysit, it is not kindergarten. You cannot babysit these people so I think it all comes down to is this person ready to commit his or herself to this kind of work or get a new job somewhere else? (Vitaly)

Vitaly's experience of life seems to be one of adaptation, he stated:

> I am trying now to find new people in my life who are ok with this, who are accepting of me. On the other

hand, I also know the sensitivity affects my relationships with people and how I react to them either in anger or any other feelings, so I am sort of also trying to work on my own feelings and the way I react to them.

Astrid, one of the participants from Denmark, related being strongly advised by her father to choose banking as a career. Her father admonished that "He has told me so many times that you have to start, you will finish, you will be nothing, you will be working the system" (Astrid). Though she did work in banking for some time Astrid described feeling an inner pull toward a career more attuned to her highly sensitive trait. In her quest for self-knowledge Astrid reports that in Denmark "there is not so many people who know about HSPs." I asked her if people are accepting of her needs if she expresses them and her reply was:

> If I tell them my needs. It is much harder but if they don't understand it I think. I am not the only highly sensitive person here in Denmark so, but I think I have not always liked that I am highly sensitive person, because it does not fit into our society. It does not fit in and I think a lot of people think the same way as I do. I think that they do not fit in and even though they can feel I need to rest now they don't listen to them self, because they don't know much about it. (Astrid)

Chouko, the participant from Japan, described how HSPs are not recognized or understood, in her words,

People didn't know anything about it. Even after I found this concept, it has been ten years now, and people do not know about it, even in psychology. I did a presentation at the conference to let them know about this. They just say maybe you are neurotic. I say I am not talking about neurotic. I said it is innate. It fits, yes to my culture. Being introvert is very accepted here. We call people shy. Shy is not a bad thing or negative here. It is just shy. Shy means we should not force her to do things or force her to speak. She is just shy. It doesn't mean negative to me or to other people. Over stimulating things that is a problem. It fits to our culture, yes, but could be neurotic. People think that highly sensitive people are neurotic, not highly sensitive or introvert. I see many highly sensitive extravert here, because they speak up. Oh, it is too bright. It is too loud. Those people probably have a more difficult time here. It is because people do not like them here.

Chouko further articulated that HSPs in Japan seem to be invisible "if there are 20 percent of highly sensitive, even in Japan say, I don't see them much. Only 10 percent that I feel are highly sensitive, maybe 20 percent, but they don't know themselves."

Adelle is primarily French Canadian, but has lived in the U.S. and France for extended periods of time. She described Canada as having better social laws, but that the people in the U.S. are "more friendly...wherever I went I met very nice people. It is important for me to be surrounded by nice people where you feel you can connect with quickly" (Adelle). Adelle disclosed that "society in Quebec is very elitist and they are very much into themselves. They are, believe it or not. I would think all Quebecers are HSP's, but in the negative sense. They are trying to protect themselves instead of opening themselves up to the world." Her purported desire is to return to the U.S. to live long-term.

Ning grew up in Taiwan then moved to the U.S. to pursue a career. She recounted how as a child "in most Chinese families, the focus is on education. My own job growing up is to do good in school. Not like the kids here. They learn so many other things growing up." Ning characterizes her life in Taiwan as "sheltered," and not having "to worry about anything else just academics." Further, she emphasizes that in Chinese culture "I always think of other people first. We never take more than we need...I like those kinds of character, we take it for granted. I am very generous. I always, very generous, whatever I can give, I give. I am like a giver, I like to give" (Ning). Ning noted that "meditation is my culture," and that cultivating a strong spiritual base is imperative to her.

Social class.

Prior to conducting this study I assumed that stratification by social class would factor prominently in my eventual interpretations. I based this on previous graduate research I conducted in my master's program on the subject of poverty. As previously noted the majority of participants in this study hold at least a bachelor's degree or higher. Of the remaining participants education is either very important to them and they have continued to learn and grow on their own without formal education, or they have at least some college. None of the participants reported a dislike or disdain for education. Participants in this study are predominantly well-educated and from the middle class. Some have progressed to the upper levels of what can be construed to be middle class, while many have not achieved as much as their education might otherwise indicate should be possible.

The majority of participants have deviated from what may be considered a typical middle-class life path of increasing achievement, remuneration, and responsibility, favoring instead a life that is more authentic and responsive to their needs as HSPs. This rejection of a static social role with predestined, prescribed norms seems to be of great importance to participants in this study. Many articulated a need for new social roles that redefine how we relate to each other.

Race.

Participants in this study are predominately White and of likely Northern European heritage, thus this study is nearly homogenous, however, two are African-American and I include this section to provide an accounting of their unique racial experiences to provide a deeper contextual setting. Guy is an African-American male from what he recounted is a "somewhat privileged" background where his needs were taken care of as long as he was "responsible, respectful, and went to college to contribute something in a meaningful way." Guy's related his experience of race,

School was tough. It was my sister and I and we were

the only black kids in our private school. In public school we were still the only two black kids. We had to learn to define ourselves as individuals very quickly because of the bicultural aspect. We had to adapt fast. Our parents would try and get us into black immersive experiences. We were neither black enough for the black kids or white enough for the white kids. We became very bicultural. My sister and I really learned how to define ourselves at a very early age, to fend off unwarranted expectations. We became very independent. I did it in kind of an isolated manner. I became the silent jock. My sister became a professional dancer.

Guy's experience of being bicultural required him to learn how to utilize his empathy to gauge other's reactions. In his words:

No, it was a survival thing being able to understand where people were coming from, being sensitive to their needs, their perspective...why they think the way they do, why they move the way they do. It was something I had to do. I had to become extremely sensitive. I had to utilize it on a day-to-day basis in order to not necessarily fit in, but to maintain some sort of credence...so the sensitivity is a necessity to this day. I walk into a room and kind of see what's going...it can change what you're going to do and how you're going to do it. (Guy)

The racial aspect of biculturalism, for Guy, forced him to

utilize empathy in a pragmatic manner. This contrasting experience was not expressed by the other African-American participant, Kurt, who instead described a home life in chaos, but with no prominent racial emphasis.

Gender.

Differing gender experiences emerged in this study early as male participants related experiencing gender role conflicts with others in their lives. Sociologically it is known that gender separates our experience of life and HSPs are no exception. Of the 11 males who participated in this study all related difficulties as their highly sensitive natures came into conflict with conventional expectations of masculinity. None of the female participants reported similar issues with expectations of femininity. In this section I present the three most significant aspects of the male experience of SPS including gender role conflicts, the male experience of androgyny, and a tentative outline for an integral masculinity that emerged from the male participants.

First, I will define the term gender and briefly outline the traditional male ideal of masculinity. Gender is a broad construct that is socially derived and culturally specific. The division by biological sex assignment is reinforced by what are known as gender role norms. Connell (1995) referred to these as hegemonic masculinity. Donaldson (1993) defined hegemonic masculinity as comprising several key characteristics males are supposed to embody including violence and aggression; emotional restraint, courage, toughness, risk-taking, competiveness, and achievement and success. Males who fail to present this version of masculinity, including gay males and males who act even slightly effeminate or who fail to completely adhere to the hegemonic view of masculinity, are subject to ridicule, shaming, and physical and emotional abuse (O'Neil, 1981; Pleck, 1981). Further, males are conditioned from a very young age to believe that aggression and lust are the only acceptable forms of expression (Zeff, 2010; Slater, 2009).

Gender role conflicts.

The males in this study comprised a cross-section of expression of masculinity. Two participants are military veterans, three played competitive sports in high school or college, four are high sensation-seeking HSPs, and one identified as gay. Additionally, eight are from unsupportive childhoods with their deviations from a full expression of hegemonic masculinity serving as a primary catalyst for emotional and physical abuse from others, particularly fathers. The participant who identified as gay, though he experienced an overall supportive childhood, reported shaming and abuse for his effeminate expression of his gender. Below are a few examples of lack of acceptance of sensitivity experienced by participants:

> It became more obvious through experience that sensitivity was something that I needed to keep to myself. It was basically a punishable offense, not in school, but with my dad. He was not respectful of that trait in me at all... I grew up with a father who was very, very hostile to who I was...It was particularly difficult for me, because being sensitive it seemed like everything I did was to slow, it was wrong, you know

just not acceptable, not what he wanted, and I had problems in school and gym classes and so forth. I seem to be kind of clumsy. I didn't really pick things up in terms of physical skills, because that is what the other boys did. I would get punished for that. Sometimes I just got shamed and struck in front of the other kids, so that made me feel stupid, like I was just incapable of doing things like that. As I got in high school, I really wanted to be part of the male peer group and so I went ahead and did sports anyway. I went out and raved and ranted and all that stuff, but it didn't come easily to me, so I could be part of a peer group. I also did a bunch of stuff that I really didn't want to do, because I didn't want to be seen as a pussy or whatever the boys put on each other. I think that in some ways I made some necessary adjustments so that I wouldn't feel ostracized, but it wasn't necessarily because I felt comfortable doing those things. (Kirk)

I tried to play in sports. I played football, but I was not, I mean, I did not like playing and I did not drive as hard as I could have and I didn't hit as hard as I could have. Almost like participating in life, but not quite...Now looking in retrospect at my life, I see that I was way over stimulated all of the time. Especially being around a father who I couldn't do anything right. He would easily spit down on me to cuss me out or take a swing on me. I got highly sensitive to my environment. It did not take much to set me off. I had a hot temper for a lot of years. I would just explode in an instant. (Joshua)

I wasn't able to make decisions quick enough, so she would scream and yell as my father would...I remember as a kid, you know, crying and my dad coming in and saying shut up and I stopped crying. He walked out and my mom said go ahead and cry...I played football for five years, which that was a challenge being who I was, because I am a big guy, I am six foot three...I remember the coach telling me to go to the game and just spit on the guy in front of me, so spit on him, and tell him that he slept with his sister. I was like, I had never had sex before, I was kind of very shy in a really big kid's body and I came out of the game and he said, did you do it. I said no, and I couldn't lie, you know. He said, "you are a nice guy Kurt and that is not good." He just walked away very disappointed with me, right... I remember that story because that is the general attitude, you know, kind of systemic around the limitations of what men can be...that is the challenge with my father, you know, with his expectations of what men should be and how he was raised. (Kurt)

Male experience of androgyny.

Androgyny is an equal expression of instrumental and expressive traits related to gender (Bem, 1974). Instrumental traits, such as aggressiveness, competitiveness, self-confidence, and logic, are thought to represent masculinity, while expressive traits, such as warmth, caring, nurturing, and sensitivity represent femininity (Shifren & Bauserman, 1996). Androgynous individuals tend to be healthier and more adaptable and resilient by virtue of their greater range of possible behaviors to act from. The male participants in this study seemed to embody instrumental and expressive traits to a roughly equal degree. Moreover, though many expressed a history of shaming and ridicule for not displaying normative, hegemonic masculine behaviors or actions, the continued integration and embodiment of both traits seemed to be a high priority.

Kurt's aforementioned description of non-acceptance of his sensitive nature caused him to continually question himself, to suffer low self-esteem, and begin to question societal conceptions of normative gender roles. In his words:

> I really believe that we embody feminine and masculine energies and I think really systemically I think the feminine has been crushed in an attempt to assassinate that within myself and also outside of yourself. I think that if we can accept those parts of ourselves and not just accept them but nurture them. I think it is like we will tolerate it, but I am not really, it is not really accepting or feeding it. I think when we do that, it can help with a lot of things. I think a lot of folks are just trapped in those kind of concepts of what a man should be and what a woman should be. (Kurt)

The view that our society has trapped us into narrow roles of "normative" versus "non-normative" was expressed by most of the participants in this study, but especially by male participants who seem to embody a broader definition of masculinity.

Embodying integral masculinity.

Participant descriptions of androgyny began to make me consider a more inclusive definition of masculinity enfolding and embracing instrumental and expressive traits. I asked Seth how he thought a new definition of masculinity might emerge. He responded as follows:

That is an interesting question. I think mostly just by succeeding. It is kind of related to, I kind of see it as the whole social spectrum like being gay used to be not terribly acceptable until people realized that they do have stuff to contribute and they are not evil. They are not going to do whatever people thought they were going to do. It never bothered me at all. I was pretty secure in my person. I think we need to get people around that knee jerk reaction that, oh, you cannot be highly sensitive and be masculine and to realize that you can be somewhat introspective and still be masculine. (Seth)

Kurt and Bruce added their interpretations of how they view androgyny and the problem of non-acceptance of sensitivity in males:

I think one of the roles is just being true to ourselves. That is a really huge to live in our bodies and our spirits, because you work in the world and I think really, you know, what you and I are doing right now kind of talking to each other about all these things and actually taking it out of the isolation and shadows. That is where it has been placed and you see me kind of dust it off and polish and put it out there. I think that leads to action. I think that leads to some kind of shift and change somehow...It makes me sad sometimes, but there are also opportunities in that to shift things and, you know, to really embody where we want to embody. (Kurt)

I tend to look at stuff on the small scale and each individual. For example, for me my relationships with the kids in the after school program was great, because in some way that was my goal to redefine masculinity with the males there and not, because they had a lot of anger there, and to just be sensitive to say, ok, well how can I just listen to them and be open to that and say, yeah, your feelings are valid or you have the right to be angry where you are at and to give them a platform to talk about that. I think if I would want to redefine masculinity that would be it, just allow males to be able to express their feelings in a way that is healing. (Bruce)

The male participants constructed a new, tentative vision of masculinity through their collective contemplativeness acknowledging their negative experiences with those subscribing to a traditional, hegemonic view of masculinity while articulating a more inclusive, synergistic, integral definition. Some experienced greater difficulty with traditional definitions of gender roles than others. Guy, for instance, developed a "tough" exterior as a football player that sheltered his inner sensitive self while he attempts to create a life honoring his inner need for meaning and his external needs to serve others and be of pragmatic utility. Bruce seems to be secure enough within himself that challenges to his masculinity are fewer than for other males who may exhibit effeminate affects. Kent described an early life of bullying, but later developed a strong resilience to criticism. Vitaly is still engaged in an ongoing process of discovering how to be a highly sensitive male in Russia, which still subscribes to a traditional view of masculinity.

Theme 8: Work

The theme of *work* is central to how HSPs experience careers. I placed it at this position to allow a space for a deeper understanding of the social context within which HSPs live; variations in how SPS is expressed individually including the self-care practices HSPs reported as essential; and to fully appreciate the complex nature of life for HSPs. The experience of work carries with it a unique cultural initiation and expectations of adherence to these cultural norms and practices. This theme elucidates several significant areas, as revealed by participants, including interpersonal aspects of work; the physical environment of work; the structure of work; and authentic work. Though these areas of emphasis repeated across participants there were contrasting views provided by some participants.

Interpersonal.

I asked all 35 participants a specific question about how interpersonal relationships affect them in their careers in order to distinguish between person-to-person interactions and stimuli from the built environment. Responses clustered along social preference lines with those participants preferring relatively low sociability expressing dislike for open office plans with forced interaction the most, while those preferring high sociability related a liking for interaction, but experiencing social fatigue if the interactions continue for too long. Many recounted a preference for a flexible sociability whereby interaction with others is interspersed with periods of quiet that enables them to focus on their work. Participants in this study largely seemed to embody qualities of introversion and extraversion. Eight participants are likely extraverts, 27 are likely introverts, while 18 of the latter seemed to be proficient at expressing an extraverted affect when expedient.

Participants in this study expressed a strong dislike for aggressive or highly competitive individuals. Further, most expressed a strong dislike for superficiality in conversation or interaction, preferring instead deeper, more meaningful interactions. Most participants detailed a strong preference for one-on-one interactions with co-workers and customers or clients. Participants also expressed that they are highly conscientious and possess a strong need for things done well by others. Finally, autonomy was strongly valued by all participants in this study. Below are some representative examples of participant responses to the aforementioned preferences:

Probably about a year ago, we did some reorganization and switched my direct supervisor and so it went from one of the better supervisors in the company to one of the weaker ones, so there has been a lot of friction since then. My boss is incompetent in his job. He can't even manage to do simple things like keeping you informed about things you are supposed to know about. It is like, you are not doing your job, which is impeding us from doing our job and causing friction. Nobody seems to care that he is bad at his job. (Seth)

It's a little draining being around people. I'm also a little introverted. So it's a little draining. Being around people all the time at work. I would like to leave the option open that's why when I do write I go to a coffee shop or something. I like to be around people, but not talking so I don't feel so inclined. But I was kind of forced into another room to talk to other teachers and chat so I hated it. (Colleen)

He was very cocky. He was a cocky man, he was just a real ass. One day he put me on the floor to work like a mental health technician, which is below a nurse, the nurses are actually responsible for these MHT's and I'm like "Oh good, I get to be an MHT for a day! And he got in my face and said "you will never be an MHT, you are a nurse, act like one!" I didn't really do anything wrong I don't think, but apparently I did. That statement and that just really overwhelmed me that I'm going to have to work with this ass you know forever and put up with this. (Hailey)

There's only one of the people in my office that's a definite extrovert...before he got his own office he was out in the main pit with the rest of us and, like a lot of extroverts, I know he thinks by talking, and he just constantly talks and constantly has to have noise, and the radio station he always wanted to listen to was one of those classic rock stations, that apparently only plays 40 songs over and over...I was so relieved when he finally got his own office away from the rest of us, I mean it was blissfully quiet. Although we can still hear him talking and he whistles sometimes when he's working on a manuscript he'll start whistling and not realize he's doing it and he'll spend all day whistling if we don't go and knock on his door and tell him to shut up. (Andrea)

I work one on one with people. Mostly it is people who have been hurt by the church. I deal with people who have experienced, what I call, religious abuse. In some ways they have been told that they are not good enough, they are not good people, by some religious authority. My goal is to help them heal from that and to find a way for them to feel that they have a connection to whatever is bigger however they need to find it. (Samantha)

That is the thing. If you had your space that you can

go and close the door and think better, because that is something I have noticed. At the volunteer place, I have my own email now and my own desk and stuff, so. When I go to work and I check my email and then like if somebody is behind me talking I can't...wouldn't be able to tell you, because I don't know what happens in my brain. I just tend to, the information does not go in when there is too much going on like people talking. I just can't concentrate. (Zoe)

All the complex emotions and stuff that can go on and frequently does go on in the workplace comes across to three or four times more strongly, and does and is that much more difficult to deal with. (Evelyn)

The interpersonal working environment can also be an inspiring place with HSPs reporting being more positively affected by supervisors and co-workers who attend to creating a positive working environment by setting the tone themselves. HSPs are deeply impacted by the intrinsic emotional energy in any space, thus in work spaces, since a large amount of time is spent in them daily, it seems critical for HSPs to have conditions conducive to concentration, focus, and lack of conflict. Below are example quotes from participants relating the effect of positive experiences involving co-workers and supervisors:

Positive stimulation is certainly a motivator. I wish all managers were as enlightened as he is. Yes, positive feedback does have an effect on me. If managers did more of it, they would get more productivity and happier employees. (Evelyn)

I had some pretty good supervisors and platoon sergeants. I had one in particular that I liked...He really wanted to learn to do his job better...He would frequently ask input from the subordinates under him...We ended up talking a lot and I told him what I thought and what was going on. He made improvements and we had a great little group of people...Over the course of probably a year and a half that I was there with him, everybody's physical training score went up, everybody's promotion scores went up. It was just a really good environment. (Seth)

We all worked together. If I was busy with a customer, somebody else could write up the sale and we worked together. The customers didn't feel like they were shark-bait and their needs came first before the needs of us working on commission...so instead of being in competition with one another, we would work together...It was a great environment. I learned a lot from them. (Taylor)

Taylor's positive experience was undermined when the owner decided to dissolve cooperation and instead pit the employees against each other for sales commissions. In Taylor's words,

He then said that we couldn't pool our commissions any more. The job environment changed...my coworker who was then my friend, who I had shared sales with, she said to me "you know Taylor, it is a new game and it is not like that anymore and I don't like you ingratiating yourself to my customers." I was really like wounded...When they changed the game, I still sold the same amount of furniture, but I didn't like my working relationship with my co-workers. It got petty and competitive and it wasn't supportive. (Taylor)

Many HSPs in this study expressed a serious concern for the tone of ultra-competitiveness they experienced in the workplace preferring instead workplaces that facilitate deep, meaningful connections with others. Many of the HSPs in this study have, either shifted some or all of their work to home-based or have opted for self-employment or plan to do so.

Physical environment.

The physical, built environment can have a significant effect on well-being and overall health. I asked each participant how the physical work environment affects them. There were several repetitive responses including dislike of open-office floor plans; preference for natural light over artificial with light levels varying from low to high; disordered work spaces; cramped work spaces, and unpleasant noises, smells and extremes of temperature. Though responses varied most participants related reacting more strongly to unsatisfactory physical conditions than their co-workers do

Structure of work.

The way work itself is structured can have a significant effect on how we are able to carry it out on a daily basis. Participants in this study articulated several consistent viewpoints including a preference for autonomous work; flexible working hours; dislike of repetition; need for mentally stimulating work; and having time to focus intently on the task at hand. The need for autonomy was expressed very strongly by participants with a strong dislike of being watched or feeling as if they are being watched while performing a task. Aubree stated she prefers a "less supervised environment...I'm very comfortable working on my own." Lily recounted how any repetitive activity "makes me nauseous." Seth's preference is to work on a "small collaborative team where I can help other people and they can help me. I just think that synergy of ideas and bouncing ideas off of one another, because it helps to have somebody there that you can ask a question of...that's where I'm at my best." Though many participants work best in quiet, like Seth, they seem to understand and appreciate the value of synergy and collaboration. Concurrent with the desire to do good work is the need for meaningful work.

Authentic work.

All of the 35 participants in this study expressed a strong need to do work that is meaningful to them and to others. Of the HSPs who reported a predominant need to protect themselves the need for meaningful work was a consistent thread. Embedded within the need for meaningful work is the underlying trait of conscientiousness reported by all 35 participants. Conscientiousness is a personality trait, but is related to achievement orientation, dependability, and orderliness (Judge, Higgins, Thoresen, Barrick, 1999). Conscientious individuals are disciplined, focused, organized, goal-oriented, deliberate in thought and action, reliable, and may be perfectionists when taken to extreme. Conscientiousness is the only trait demonstrated to reliably predict success at work. Below are representative quotes of participant responses citing conscientiousness:

> What I've heard over and over..."you're very conscientious," and I think that's why they like me so much because, as a nurse, people die with people who aren't conscientious. (Hailey)

> I am very quality-oriented and if that means I step on peoples toes, I step on peoples toes and people don't appreciate that...When you are an HSP and very conscientious and work forced it is very easy for coworkers to feel like we are unfriendly or aloof. I got that often. When they would tell you anything at all, it was that. Mostly they wouldn't tell you and just acted. So I was frequently very isolated (Evelyn)

> I am always proud that I have never screwed over a customer intentionally...I never did anything with malice and I gave great service. (Ava)

> I want things done, I mean work environment was ok, but I demand more and people cannot understand...I can do much more than I expected myself or definitely

what other people expect me to do. Very fast and very accurate. I like to have things done before the due date or so people respect me in a way, even never having a full-time job. They always ask me to stay. (Chouko)

On occasion we are told to do something that we know is wrong, and we will bring it up and they will say, oh just do it anyway. It doesn't matter. Six months later it blows up and they are like, oh my god, it's the end of the world and I am like, well I told you six months ago that this was going to happen. We kind of know, or at least I do mostly because I have training. I look a little deeper and see what the repercussions are...When I am writing something I like to keep it more simple, readable, and maintainable. (Seth)

I began to understand that participants have an intrinsic need to do a job well, but also to ensure their hard work has meaning beyond the task itself and beyond oneself. Below are several representative quotes encapsulating participant's need for meaningful work:

In my case I started fighting the system when I was ten about what I was going to do and how I was going to do it and I am still fighting. To know that it is worth fighting for and that in your heart you are doing the right thing. That is the self-motivating part. (Samantha)

I know I could never work at a job that did not meet

my values, my personal values. I just can't do it. I could have...made a ton of money, but I didn't respect my boss, I didn't like the tension between my co-workers, and I just have to be in a place where I feel healthy, physically healthy, mentally healthy, emotionally healthy...I can't break myself up into pieces for prestige or money or even security. (Taylor)

I take great pride in what I am doing. I can, I don't know if this is part of an HSP or what, but I feel really good about the amount of care I take with my work and the fact that even though I am doing the dictation and taking care of a person's medical record, that I feel what I do really makes a difference in that person's care. (Faith)

Faith also recounted what she termed her "greatest professional achievement." I present this lengthy quote as an illustration of one instance in which a HSP found true meaning and fulfillment in her work,

> I had a client, he has passed away now, who had profound mental retardation. He had severe contractures of his limbs. A contracture if you are not familiar with it, is where the muscles and ligaments have pulled so tightly that the limb is fixed. It's almost like it is so spasmed that it won't move out of that position. This individual, William, he was, I mean he had the IQ was maybe that of a two year old at best. He was essentially nonverbal. He was about fifty. He was in a wheelchair most of the time. He could not

move himself in that wheelchair. He could get up a little bit. His feet were really swollen. He could do a little bit of getting up from his wheelchair over to a couch and he had some other behavior difficulties. One of the things he would do was to cry out a lot, probably we guessed in frustration. He would bite his hand. He had severe calluses on his hand from biting on it so bad. Well, one of the things we decided as a team was that it might help William and perhaps make him feel less frustrated if he could learn to propel himself in his wheelchair. The group home was a large ranch style home. It was like six bedrooms on one side and a huge living room and then a long kitchen. If you put like two ranch-style homes together, and had all that length that is what it would be like. We decided that would be a good idea and if we could get William and teach him to self-propel. He only had one hand he could really, well he had two if he didn't bite on one. His fists were kind of clutched. If we could get him to self-propel fifteen feet in a year, that would be doing really good. Well, I wrote up part of my thing was to write up the steps of the teaching module to get William to do this. I would also work with the person who worked with him, so I enjoyed doing it. hat was one of my favorite things to do. I looked at it, looked at his trainer, worked with it, and figured out what to do. We then would go back sometimes and revise the steps as we saw what he was able to do and what he wasn't. Well, it just so happened that one day William got stuck and propelled himself a little bit and he got stuck in the corner by the water fountain by my office. I happened to hear him and he was moaning and I came out and said, "William, what is the matter?" I said, "Ok, William let's back out. I am going to show you." I did hand-over-hand with him and I showed him how to back out, this was not in his plan at all to back out of that corner. At first he didn't get it, and I showed him again (hand-over-hand) and then he started, now mind you this is an individual with the age of a two year old ok. I...showed him with his hand under mine to back it up and there I asked him to do it. He tried. This took a few minutes and finally he got the hang of it and I said, "good, do it again," and he got it. I then said, "do it with the other hand, go forward," and showed him that way and he backed it out of that corner. I said, "go forward," and I showed him that way, and all of the training I had been doing for two months snapped together and he went from one side of the house to another. He never got stuck in the corner again. It was wonderful. William just let out the biggest laugh you had ever heard. I just about cried. I was like, "oh my god William!" All the trainers came out and I said, "look what William did!" and William was just laughing out loud. I said, "oh god William, that is wonderful!" I said, "Look at you! You did it!" I said, "you can go anywhere now." The hand biting after that went way down. He was able to wheel himself all over the house. He didn't go fifteen feet, he went thirty he went all over. He never got caught in that corner again. He just increased his quality of life by oodles. I was so proud of myself. I was so proud of him. That has stuck in my life as one of the best professional things I have ever done. I just feel so privileged to be part of that individual's life and to help him. You just don't get moments like that very often. (Faith)

The need to engage in meaningful, life-affirming work that fulfills participant needs for conscientiousness and altruism represents an attitude toward life beyond superficialities and social class expectations. I reflected on the aforementioned themes at length before arriving at the final theme.

Theme 9: The Integral Being

The final tentative theme is *meta* in nature and coalesced late in my interpretations. One of the most strongly expressed feelings about being a HSP is that there is "something wrong with us." This perception was expressed repetitively by most of the participants and seems to represent a deep-seated belief formed through conflict with social norms. In order to challenge this belief one must engage in an extensive internal and external reappraisal process requiring radical challenges to cultural programming. What is considered normative in one culture may be non-normative in another, thus a definition of normative is relative to one's culture. The process of questioning and reevaluating one's perceptions in a search for "faulty" cultural beliefs, beliefs intrinsically exclusionary and narrowly focused, are a part of the overall process of creating culture that we are all continually engaged in, consciously or unconsciously. The phrase "canary in the coal mine" was another prominent elucidation of the role many HSPs feel they can play within society as they challenge social norms and potentially redefine them.

HSPs in this study, cumulatively, seem to have articulated a vision for a way of life that is inherently more authentic to their personality trait. Authenticity in this instance seems to mean a way of being that honors the role of empathy, intuition, and a rich, complex inner life; radical self-care; creativity and high sensation-seeking; a broadened definition of gender roles (specifically androgyny); interpersonal and physical working conditions that respect the needs of all people; and reframing and refocusing one's life as a means of service to others, while cultivating a sense of being *totally awake*. By totally awake I mean a sense of complete awareness rooted in the present moment where participants have integrated and accepted the parts of themselves that society deems to be deviant. Deviant here means diverging from what is considered normative by customary social norms. Carl Jung's concept of individuation seems an especially appropriate method of personal growth and development for what participants have expressed in this study. Embracing the elements we have pushed into the *shadows* may lead us to a greater integration of self with significant implications for our society as we withdraw projections from others and embody an integral sense of being. In this theme I present a tentative, emergent vision of the integral being.

Cultivating self-awareness and radical self-acceptance.

HSPs, by their intrinsic nature seem to be very deep-thinking, sensitive individuals with a keen awareness of themselves and others. Many, however, may attempt to hide away their sensitive side as societal pressures to conform and display the appropriate affect is applied. This rejection of a personality trait that may pervade every part of one's experience of life may create an imbalance in the individual's psyche that cannot be resolved until the choice is made to confront these shadow elements. In Jungian theory this integration process may take many years, even a lifetime. Individuals engaging in this process may experience denial, emotional discomfort, and pain as they discover long-hidden aspects of themselves. Joshua described his orientation toward total awakeness in this way:

> In the last ten years and especially more now than ever, motivated by consciousness. I am motivated by increasing my own awareness and through that awareness changing my life and handling what that change looks like. That is my sense of motivation. I couldn't say career, money, live life, you know none of that any more. That was one of the things I clung to in the past, but they don't mean that much anymore. Being completely in my body and sensitized where I am 100 percent present is the most important.

Olivia expressed a gentle and kind way of encountering and embracing the aspects of herself that contradict her self-conception:

I would definitely say getting to know oneself is the most important thing, and also being willing to be surprised just in the sense that through acknowledging that I am highly sensitive and introverted. I have also been able to encounter the part of me that is more outgoing or vivacious and that I can play with that and that sometimes my personality can be a contradiction and that it is ok to be in that connection and not creating tension...getting to know oneself, and then being willing to be surprised. For me having a very genuine, honest relationship with myself is important.

The willingness to accept parts of ourselves that clash with societal and personal norms is not without risk, yet, as Julia articulated "the other thing that I have done was just accept, pure acceptance. I ended up, what I wrote in my journal was this is it, I am who I am already. It is not going to change at this point. Let's just live who you are and stop trying to figure out how to self-improve." Self-help books proliferate the shelves of bookstores with advice on how to change various aspects of ourselves, yet what Julia proposes is a radical self-acceptance. Many participants related that being a HSP has been difficult for them. Julia again relates:

You have to accept who you are. That means your strengths and your weaknesses, your shadows and your dark sides and not try to suppress them and try to say, well, these are my issues in life and I need to work with this or how do I work with this? How do I work with that and around it and direct my life that way and not pretend that it is not part of you.

The aforementioned sense of risk entailed in getting to know and accept oneself does not automatically impart personal transformation leading to any guaranteed improvement in self-concept. This may be especially true for those HSPs who experienced an unsupportive childhood because early tendencies toward fear and anxiety may prevent or impair them from a fuller realization of potentialities. Olivia shared how accepting that she is a HSP was "incredibly liberating," but that she also:

> did not want to hold it too preciously...If we only see ourselves through that lens, it is like we can sort of cocoon ourselves more and want to control everything of our lives and so there is a sense of releasing the pressure of it...and to be able to own it or embody it in a confident way and invite people into that...Once I was able to relax into that, it just kind of brought confidence into my life.

Olivia's description of "inviting others" into her confident, relaxed embodiment of SPS with its "capacity to range across human expression" seems to imply that she has integrated SPS well enough to access a way of being that holistically allows her to flourish and be able to effectively contribute to society in deep, meaningful ways.

Learning to thrive.

Participants in this study are at various points in their journeys of acceptance and learning to thrive, but the cumulative intention seems to be one desiring a state of optimal functioning or *flow*. By thriving I mean to be in a state where one's capacities are fully engaged and directed toward goals that mesh with personal and professional goals in a sustainable manner. To reach this state individuals need to have spent significant time developing self-awareness and have accepted themselves as they are. A minority of HSPs seem to have reached this state, but most are actively engaged in the process of learning to thrive. Guy related how his approach to life is rooted in service:

> I don't think you can hold the sensitive space that we do without a desire to share it. Being able to find a way to be of service, otherwise I don't have much motivation, yeah, I really don't. If I can't really contribute in some sort of meaningful way there's not much else to do but read and have some tea and contemplate and have a few good conversations. I live a really simple life. We've only gotten here together, so regardless of the hierarchy of our togetherness, there's a large role for the contemplative approach that would rather listen to a hundred different perspectives and try and connect the dots and allow their inspiration to come in, that's what creativity is. It's those "aha" moments that happen universally. They want to have step-by-step instructions to intuition, it doesn't work like that. It's much more non-linear. Like step one is clear your mind, good luck with that, you know?

Lucy explained her approach to thriving is based in

helping others learn to thrive:

> I am big on finding your natural talent, so I encourage
> people to first do some passion finding and figure out
> what their values and what they need to make them
> feel complete and feel joy then talk about their natural
> talents, and then take those natural talents and find a
> job where they are not feeling like they are swimming
> upstream all the time. It should be easier, your job
> should be an extension of you that helps you operate
> from ease and not always piddling upstream

Linda provided a succinct elucidation regarding our society's
focus on our external selves:

> Now that we have more or less gotten rid of people's
> interiors, instead of knowing a person's interior, I
> kind of think that society prefers just to deal with
> extraverts so people can talk a lot and show what
> might be in their exteriors instead. So, it's kind of
> doing something superficial rather than doing
> something deep...in other cultures, especially Asian
> cultures, they tend to be sensitive to the environment
> and to be more quiet and introverted and it is actually
> valued. That would be good.

The emphasis on contemplativeness, introspection,
intuition, and empathy by participants in this study seems to
create a space where a new, more integral being may
flourish. Though the majority of HSPs may attain a
semblance of the integral being several participants provided
a glimpse into what it might resemble:

Somebody needs to see the beauty that is here. Somebody needs to cry for those who can't cry for themselves. Somebody needs to laugh for those who can't laugh...that's a weird gift. It is a strange privilege. (Faith)

My whole motivation is that I don't want other people to live the life I have had to. I want them to have a better shot. I sort of fight for at least my little corner to be a nicer place. (Samantha)

I would say that people who are oriented to integrating that kind of contemplative, spacious reflective, thoughtful tier of life into a kind of action-oriented society is incredibly necessary. (Olivia)

I think with more understanding, like if I am to understand myself I have to have a sense of myself and then I understand that I don't have to fit into other people's world, people are different. Everyone is different, so what they want I may not want. This need to be sensitive, to know what it means and accept that people are different. I am different and other people are different from me so there is no right and wrong. It is just different and accepting myself and others. Understanding is one thing, trying to remember is another thing. I think that is the most difficult part. We just have to keep on reminding ourselves, that is why I think meditation is so important. It helps me to remember. We have to find ourselves first, find a boundary. Like a structured home base and from there you can go out to the world to do things to help. (Ning)

I think we are here to transform. I think we are the ones who are called upon...to start without being aggressive because it is not necessarily in our nature to be aggressive to keep our stand and say, no, no, no, this is not the way to make things work. I think it is our time to start showing other people that non HSP's or even people that there are other ways. I think HSP's are actually an opening for other people. (Adelle)

Conclusion

This chapter began with a description of the participants in this study. I included a brief summary of demographic characteristics including a breakdown by gender, nationality, age, educational level, and occupation, to situate the participants in a context. I then outlined the nine themes identified in the data analysis phase. Following that I presented full results from each theme with a narrative and supporting quotes from participants. In chapter five I present an extensive discussion of these results along with limitations of the study and future research implications as well as a conclusion to the entire study.

CHAPTER 5

DISCUSSION AND CONCLUSION

The purpose of this study was to better understand the way HSPs experience careers. To accomplish this it was necessary to better understand the way HSPs experience life. The interview protocol was written to cover a broad spectrum of lived experience. The interviews were richer than I had hoped for and yielded poignant and informative information detailing every aspect of life, but with a special emphasis on how these factors influenced the working life of HSPs. Thirty-five semi-structured interviews yielded nine major themes. Each theme may contain sub-themes that were either integral to the major theme or subsumed into the theme during the data analysis process. In this chapter I present a discussion of each theme organized in accordance with the themes explicated in chapter four. Following discussion of the themes I articulate some of the implications for future research involving HSPs, limitations of this study and some personal reflections on the impact of this study on my role as a researcher and on my personal life.

Discussion of Results for Theme 1: Empathy

The experience of empathy emerged as the most important theme that seemed to define what it means to be a HSP. In this limited study participants expressed two main points regarding empathy. First, empathy can be unwanted and difficult to manage, especially in social situations where one must absorb the energy of a room full of people or a crowd. Empathy, for participants means they take on the energy of others whether they wish to or not. This aspect of empathy, of constantly absorbing the energy of others or of a place, differentiates HSPs quite dramatically from the rest of the population, who may feel similar forces, but do not process them as deeply. HSPs at work must absorb energies the entire day and, with the currently popular trend of open-office floor plans, this may prove to be exhausting for a HSP who is high in empathy leading to a strong desire to leave a position or find a workable compromise such as telecommuting for part of the workday or week. Some HSPs are extraverts, however and would likely enjoy the intensive interaction to a point, but they too find themselves exhausted or overwhelmed and need to withdraw to a quiet place to recharge.

The second main point is that empathy can be an advantage. Participants described how their ability to take the other person's position proved to be advantageous in sales, customer service and in leadership where it might be desirous to know in advance the extent to which co-workers or employees are engaging and understanding the task at hand. Seth mentioned this in his capacity as a trainer. He is able to feel if one of his trainees is simply not "getting it," and change his approach. This ability would be a great advantage to anyone serving in a teaching or leadership capacity. I have noted this advantage personally as a college professor.

Andrea may have described the experience of empathy best by stating she is a "chameleon" who picks up on the mood that is being given off by others or by a place.

This chameleon-like quality separates HSPs in a fairly significant way because the stimulation is more deeply processed than for others, thus HSPs are more deeply affected by empathy and may find a situation with negative energies overwhelming well beyond what it might be for others. The same may be said of positive energy. HSPs reported generally being deeply affected by positive energy. Dale described his need to be able to discern problematic expressions he notes on the faces of his church performance groups. HSPs, in this sense, must develop capacities to distinguish across the normal range of human expressions, not assuming every expression that appears negative is necessarily problematic.

Morgan introduced a moral component to empathy as she was required to sell to the general public. In her sales capacity she was forced to choose between aggressive sales tactics and her need to respect other people's boundaries. HSPs in sales positions may find themselves with a moral dilemma; do they use their capacity for feeling what their customer is feeling to close the sale or do they respect the boundaries of the customer and find a more interested prospect? Taylor mentioned that she can sometimes use her strong empathy for manipulative purposes. This moral component is one that HSPs would need to address if they are in a position where empathy may be potentially misused.

Employers with HSPs on staff should be aware of the needs of their employees to not constantly face a barrage of emotional energy thinking creativity happens when people are in forced close conditions. Many people may find this distracting, exhausting and counterproductive to the employer's intended purpose. I suggest that, where possible, employees be allowed to "create" their own spaces in ways that feel comfortable to them. This includes physical separation between co-workers. The establishment of a separate quiet space might also prove to be advantageous for those who require a period of down time to recharge or to focus intently on a project. Telecommuting also seems a viable option to offer employees, especially HSPs, if practical. In situations where this is not practical it would be advisable to understand and appreciate the diversity of one's employees and not attempt to require conformity to a homogenous ideal. In some cases this may not be practical and it is up to each individual to experiment to an extent with various positions within a career field to find one that is acceptable with regards to the level of emotional energy one is required to absorb.

Hailey provided an insight into how this might work when she described her career as a nurse. She began her nursing career working in a mental health facility, but soon realized she needed a different environment and moved through positions in hospitals, nursing homes, rehabilitation centers, and a school district before discovering home health care. In home health care she is able to focus on a one-on-one basis and manage the level of emotional energy she is required to absorb. Not every HSP will need to go through as many permutations as Hailey, but the idea is clear; one needs to be flexible enough to make any necessary moves until the right "fit" is attained. This process may be easier for those HSPs who possess an advanced education than for those with some college or less. In those instances where survival is the overriding consideration many participants raised the possibility of self-employment. With telecommuting options at many employers, flexible working options, and self-employment there may be possibilities for those with less than a college degree. In some cases learning a trade may be a better option than a professional career.

In light of the research on empathy, especially Aron et al. (2012), the advantage of responsivity in the working world seems less of an asset than it might be in the historical context of the human species. HSPs, when viewed as approximately one-fifth of the species equipped with the ability to notice subtle differences in a number of respects, are seemingly at a disadvantage in many of the careers participants reported. For HSPs in the modern world the emphasis seems to be on the instrumental traits, which tend to value accomplishing goals in the most efficient manner possible. Empathy, in that sense, requires time and money making it less attractive in the workplace. However, some HSPs reported the usefulness of their high empathy (Hailey, Seth, and Taylor). Thus, on a macro level empathy seems to be costly and inefficient to the corporate business model, while on the micro level empathy seems to be a vital component of effective technical and interpersonal execution of work duties.

Discussion of Results for Theme 2: Childhood's Influence

The influence of early support or non-support in the lives of HSPs represents a dividing line in how participants in this study experience careers. Several expected outcomes were supported including increased likelihood of anxiety, depression, and other psychological or psychosomatic illnesses for those who experienced unsupportive childhoods; better than average functioning for those who experienced supportive childhoods; and the importance of an accepting and validating early social environment.

One unexpected, but interesting outcome of this study is that for those who experienced an unsupportive childhood they may still experience a high degree of career success. Joshua reported having an unsupportive father, yet was able to serve in the military and complete two college degrees, as well as develop a psychodrama therapeutic practice for many years. Kurt also related a chaotic home environment, which led him to explore psychology in college in search of a better understanding of his family's dysfunctions and to find ways of healing himself. This theme of individuals from unsupportive backgrounds entering the helping professions as a form of self-therapy was common among participants in this study. I was especially interested in how well these individuals were able to find appropriate careers due to my own partially invalidating childhood.

Among the participants who had supportive childhoods one of the major findings of this study seems to emphasize the importance of parental modeling of a spiritual practice. Olivia related how her parent's commitment to a strong, spiritual practice was one of the most important and influential things in her life. Ning also described spiritual practice as the basis for her life. The form a spiritual practice takes does not seem to matter, just that one has a daily spiritual practice that provides a calming, centering influence which one may return to in times of stress. A supportive childhood seems to impart a resilience that allows and enables individual explorations in the world with less fear and anxiety than for those from unsupportive childhoods. This resilience is especially important to HSPs because they are more deeply affected by negative experiences than others. This protective armoring, combined with a spiritual practice, does not seem to guarantee that one will ultimately do better than others, but that there will likely be less fear about trying new things or encountering new situations. In a career context this may translate to greater flexibility in career mobility, personal and professional career growth, and overall openness to new experience.

A supportive childhood, while supportive of resilient functioning in the individual, may also entail setting high expectations that some HSPs may struggle against as they experience conflicts in a working environment, thus hindering their ability to achieve on a conventional level. Emily reported being in a gifted program in school and achieving what might be considered significant accomplishments like speaking before a crowd of 1,000 and graduating summa cum laude from college. Emily's need to connect deeply with others and exercise a degree of creative freedom clashed with the conventional expectations of her employers. She still maintains a strong desire to achieve, yet must balance that need with her emotional needs as a HSP. This seems to indicate that HSPs need to better understand their needs at an earlier age and allow that knowledge to guide the type of career they choose. At least five HSPs in this study identified as gifted. All five related difficulties with fulfilling the expectations giftedness implies.

Previous research distinguishing between supportive and unsupportive early environments has largely emphasized the distinction itself (Aron & Aron, 1997). This study's tentative findings suggest that early environment plays a major role, but that individual choice to alter the destructive and harmful patterns learned in childhood can be mitigated to an extent. This is of great importance to HSPs who experienced unsupportive or partially unsupportive childhoods. The resilience noted in many of the participants also seems to lend credence to Possible Selves Theory (Markus & Nurius, 1986). One of the primary motivators noted in many of the participants from unsupportive backgrounds was a desire to model patterns of parental behavior toward their own children that were different from what they experienced. Thus, avoiding a possible self that is undesirable, while attempting to create a new possible self, based on moral choices.

Discussion of Results for Theme 3: Self-Care

The extent and importance of self-care is a major finding of this study. The role of self-care, as articulated by participants, is crucial and needs to begin at an early age. As aforementioned the inclusion of a spiritual practice imparts the greatest armoring effect, which serves as a refuge or home base one may return to in times of stress. The need for a dedicated spiritual practice seems to run counter to the prevailing trend toward a lessening of the interior lives that Linda mentioned, however the protective effects are significant and an addressing of attending to our spiritual lives as a society seems to be in order. Future research could explore the way spiritual practices increase resilience and inform an approach to life that is more centered or balanced on a holistic level.

The need to protect oneself, as expressed by Hailey, Joshua, and others in this study, is a poignant and tangible representation of how difficult life and work may be for some HSPs. The experience of early dysfunction again seems to predict a strong need to shield oneself from further abuse or neglect with some HSPs struggling with anxiety and trust issues long-term. The emotional damage that can be done to HSPs is staggering. The long-term implications of feeling one has no choice but to withdraw into an inner world, as expressed by Samantha, Hailey, and Julia, where fear, anxiety, and depression pervade drastically limits the fulfillment of human potential these individuals possess. These three individuals seemed to me to be highly intelligent, capable, and passionate, yet tinged with early and ongoing psychological and psychosomatic damage. Future research could address these types of emotional issues specifically geared toward healing HSPs. I was deeply touched by several of the participant's descriptions of struggles with depression, anxiety, self-medication issues, and emotional trauma, yet inspired by the spirit they expressed to help others and find peace within themselves.

Specific self-care practices varied by individuals with yoga identified as very helpful for some and other forms of physical exercise preferred by others. All acknowledged the need for a connection to nature, quiet periods of rest, adequate sleep, and a healthy diet. I realized in compiling this theme that self-care took many forms and went beyond basic issues as outlined above. Kent related how he has to carefully manage his emotional reactivity in public, by exercising a high degree of self-awareness regarding his emotions. In some cases he has to withdraw from a situation to avoid intolerable overexcitability. Joshua described a similar practice, terming the point at which he recognizes overexcitability as when his "fuse is lit." In this sense self-care becomes a spiritual practice requiring a deep knowledge of one's emotions and tendencies. It is only through careful management that many HSPs are able to function. Faith described her life as "complicated in every way." The continuous absorption of the energy of others may be overwhelming for many HSPs and may lead to a desire to withdraw from certain social interactions, lessened patience with superficiality or crowded situations –as described by Joshua– and a strong need to avoid aggressive or negative individuals.

Olivia related a gentler approach to self-care that involves getting to know oneself in a forgiving manner. In her view there will be times when she will "hit the wall" (Olivia) and know she has pushed herself beyond the point where she can effectively function. In those cases she described being willing to forgive herself for pushing her boundaries. Olivia also related a playfulness at getting to know herself and being willing to be surprised by what she can do. While it may be critical to practice self-care for HSPs it can also be limiting and confining. Olivia provides a vision for self-exploration based in the joy of discovering aspects of oneself through activities like dance, writing, and travel. In this sense self-care is a self-discovery process as much as self-protective.

Caring for oneself on a holistic level that includes physical, emotional, and spiritual needs seems to offer the most promise for HSPs. Neglect of one seems to come at the cost of imbalance to the other. The importance HSPs in this study attached to self-care helped me realize that career choice requires an alignment of the holistic needs of HSPs with career aspirations and demands. If HSPs serve the societal role of "canaries in the coal mine" what alarms are being raised with regards to the demands of work? The modern workplace's emphasis on competitiveness, aggression, enthusiasm, and dominance (Anderson et al., 2001; Hogan & Hogan, 1991; Anderson & Kilduff, 2009; Barry & Stewart, 1997) seems to be antithetical to the typical HSP orientation of observance, reflection, introspection, creativity, and cooperation. The sense of burnout noted by many of the participants seemed to play a significant role in their decisions to leave positions and seek new ones. The cumulative effect of leaving multiple positions may be very damaging to the individual's sense of self-esteem, personal confidence, explanatory style, and willingness to continue trying to find an appropriate position.

Wilcock (1993) connected individual effort to a significant engagement of capacities through occupation. This seems to indicate much of the problem lies in our post-modern approach to work. Without a necessary and significant engagement of capacities boredom, burnout, and alienation regarding the purpose of work may arise. The cumulative toll on an individual's psyche may be enormous, even leading to somatic symptoms such as fibromyalgia, anxiety, depression, and overall poor health, as reflected in participant respondents. Stress in the workplace represents a significant aspect of the experiences related by HSPs in this study. The need for self-care is a necessity that may not be fully appreciated by Americans due to the cultural emphasis on the aforementioned corporate culture of efficiency, competitiveness, and aggression. If HSPs serve an early warning function in our society due to their sensitivity the aforementioned concerns may be of great importance for the general population as well and indicate a need to address the human cost related to an unrestrained emphasis on the profit motive. Chronic underutilization of capacity has also led many HSPs to consider, or actually go, into self-employment as a means to satisfy their specific and unique needs.

Discussion of Results for Theme 4: Rich Inner Life

The inner lives of HSPs are complex and rich with variety. Viktor Frankl alluded to the value of a rich inner life in his description of those who could retreat to an inner world and who were the most resilient in the Nazi concentration camps he was interned in during World War II (Frankl, 1984). I created an umbrella theme to encompass the complexity inherent in participant descriptions. The first major sub-theme in this theme is sensory. Sensory stimulation was expected to be a major factor for HSPs in careers. Participants reported sensitivities to noises; smells; extremes of temperature; crowds; fabrics; lotions; and lights.

The reports varied from person to person with some reporting an extreme dislike of bright light, while at least one reported liking bright, natural light and strong colors. Similar fluctuations were reported with the remaining items. Some participants are bothered by bright lights and not bothered by fabrics or smells, while others dislike all of them. The sensitivities do not seem to be attributable to childhood, social class, or any other factor. All participants related at least some sensitivities, most identified with 90 percent or more of the aforementioned items as bothersome.

The cumulative impact of sensitivities to the external environment in the form of unpleasant stimulation or distractions are major issues for the HSPs in this study. I asked the participants if they noticed that they seem to be bothered by sensitivities more deeply than the people around them, all responded affirmatively. This aspect of the inner lives of HSPs primarily addresses the negative, but many participants expressed that sensory stimulation can be desirable. While HSPs are susceptible to certain trigger stimuli if they choose to be stimulated they have a greater capacity for enjoyment due to the deeper processing in the brain.

In the workplace this is a complex and complicated issue because, depending on the industry or nature of the business, unwanted stimuli may be unavoidably present. Some issues with unpleasant or overstimulation may be reasonably addressed by employers such as changing from fluorescent lighting to natural lighting or eliminating an unpleasant smell or distracting noise. In most cases participants have reported employers do not seem to be interested in meeting their needs. As discussed in theme three burnout can result from cumulatively stressful working conditions (Fernet et al., 2010). This seems to apply equally to the sensory environment, which can be noisy, dusty, dirty, chaotic, crowded, improperly lit, and overstimulating in a general sense. Though HSPs may not all be susceptible to the same sources of sensory overstimulation many are bothered by one or more to a greater extent than others.

The second major sub-theme is the love of learning expressed by participants. Though most participants related responses alluding to a love of learning several expressed just the opposite. Julia's unsupportive, neglectful childhood, combined with a career choice as a nurse seems to have effectively stymied her interest in learning. Interestingly, this is true for Julia on the job, but not in her private life, where she wants to pursue her interests in writing and landscaping. The majority of participants said learning and being afforded opportunities to learn new skills on the job were very important to them as well as personal growth and development on and off the job. This love of learning seems to be at odds with sensitivities and the need to protect oneself. Employers may view individuals expressing sensitivities as neurotics or problem-employees and ignore the complexity of personality. For employees being passed over for promotions or not utilized to their full potential may be demoralizing and defeating. The current paradigm expressed by participants, however seems to preclude significant appreciation of complex individuals in favor of conformity and predictability.

The love of learning expressed by participants

represents an intrinsic need for many HSPs. Fulfillment of intrinsic needs, as articulated by Deci and Ryan (2000), is a stronger motivator than extrinsic needs, due to the perception that intrinsic needs align with an individual's inner desires. This contention seems to be supported in this study. HSPs reported greater satisfaction when they were able to combine personally meaningful capabilities with the needs of a task (Claire and Sandy) in ways that allowed them to create something new.

The last sub-theme is complexity of thought. Along with a love of learning is deep complexity of thought. Participants described a liking for big picture thinking that incorporates the long-term. This capacity seems highly desirable in any organization, but if one is thought of as a neurotic or problem employee it is not likely the opportunities are offered to demonstrate these capacities. This seems to concur with Bendersky and Shaw's (2013) assertion that others may lower expectations of those they perceive to be "too quiet" (p. 310). The relative silence many HSPs demonstrate may be tied to social introversion, shyness, or complexity of thought. HSPs in this study reported a need for time and space to think. Concurrent with complexity is a strong dislike for superficiality related by participants. I suggest this dislike of superficiality is a reaction to the constant processing of stimulation. When one's mind is occupied by processing so much stimulation mental, exhaustion may be a real consideration. Preferring to defer only to meaningful conversation may act as an energy conservation measure. Participants mentioned a strong dislike for repetitive tasks that seems to mirror this dislike of superficiality, however repetition can also be meditative and potentially "safer" than encountering new projects on a continuous basis. This may be especially useful for HSPs with anxiety.

Discussion of Results for Theme 5: Creativity

Creativity has only been implied as being consistent with HSPs in the past. One of the major findings of this study correlates HSPs and creativity. Approximately 90 percent of participants in this study are likely creative individuals. The definition used to make that determination comprised a broad view of creativity as more than a simplistic view of creativity as those individuals involved in the arts. I decided to look beyond the surface definition of creativity in an attempt to discern the creative disposition that underlies all creative acts. Many participants described themselves as creative and working on various projects, but writing stood out as one cited repeatedly. Many of the HSPs in this study have a desire to write a book or engage in the writing process for various reasons. One is for self-care, as elucidated by Olivia in her descriptions of a writing practice that augments her other spiritual practices. A second is to produce a book that fulfills a HSP's need to achieve a tangible, societally-acceptable measure of fulfilling one's potential. Lastly, writing seems to engage the need for complex thought that many participants expressed.

Curiosity is a major component of creativity with an underlying interest and openness to new experience as the basis from which to entertain new ideas and concepts (Csikszentmihaly, 1996; Barron, 1995; Storr, 1993). Curiosity and openness to new experience were apparent in the interviewing process as participants and I explored each new question or pursued interesting divergences. HSPs may be at their best when exploring because they are able to pick up on subtle cues before others or notice things others completely miss. Creativity is often about seeing in a new way or noticing details or nuance others miss. For HSPs this natural preference for curiosity should represent an extremely valuable trait for employers. HSPs may make the best quality control inspectors or managers because of their questioning natures. HSPs may also do quite well when allowed to engage their capacities for complex thought and "big picture" orientation. The HSPs in this study, however reported that employers often did not provide those opportunities or utilize these capacities in any meaningful way. This feeling of underutilization was expressed by many participants and seems to tentatively explain the aforementioned propensities for anxiety, depression, and lack of psychological energy many participants reported (Maslow, 1968; Broeck, Vansteenkiste, DeWitt & Lens, 2010).

Participants described a sense of organizational fear of creativity whereby a "token" or superficial acknowledgement of the need to employ creative individuals manifests within organizations or companies. I suggest that creative individuals, due to their lack of predictability and the ambiguity within which they inherently operate, causes a sense of lack of control over the creative process that encourages anxiety about creativity and creative individuals. Linda related a similar experience of employers stating that they wanted creativity but "not that much creativity." Understanding this fear seems advisable and potentially useful as companies and organizations respond to changes in the global marketplace that require novel approaches to remain competitive.

Discussion of Results for Theme 6: High Sensation-Seeking

The number of high sensation-seeking HSPs in this study was unexpected and illuminating. I planned no specific questions in the interview protocol to identify HSS/HSPs, yet at least eight identified as such with at least two more being likely high sensation-seekers. This was particularly interesting to me due to my own identification as a HSS/HSP. There were several main elements that emerged from my analysis of the HSS/HSP's responses. The first is the threat of boredom. Boredom here means a state of mind where one has disengaged due to lack of interest, meaningfulness, or inherent worth of a task. Boredom seems to be a state of alienation which the HSS/HSPs in this study would do anything to avoid. Chouko related how she avoids long-term positions just to avoid boredom and burnout. Bruce described how he prefers short-term projects to avoid boredom, and Taylor portrayed boredom as her "worst enemy." Boredom, lack of interest, and burnout, as described previously, seems to be magnified for HSS/HSPs.

The second major element is curiosity and love of exploring. In HSPs curiosity has been noted as important, in HSS/HSPs curiosity and a need to explore are magnified and occupy a position of greater prominence. For HSS/HSPs the drive to explore seems almost irresistible. Many described it as a tug-of-war between their high sensation-seeking side that wants to push forward and explore, while their highly sensitive side wants to observe, use caution, and limit the exposure to stimulation. Joshua described being a HSS/HSP as "running down the street with your hair on fire."

The HSS/HSPs in this study represented the most creative and driven participants as they related involvement in multiple projects. I found their descriptions of being a HSS/HSP to parallel my lived experiences. This segment of the HSP population has not been studied before, thus the presence and identification of approximately one-third of the participants in this study as high sensation-seekers is significant. Understanding how to accommodate the needs of HSS/HSPs, and reap the benefits of driven creativity, could potentially be of great value to an organization or company. However, these individuals also seem to have a stronger need for an alignment of personal ethics with their work. Taylor described several employers who blatantly violated ethical standards in pitting employees against each other. HSPs strongly dislike competition and conflict, likely due to the depth of processing, and will react commensurately to manipulation or coercion.

HSS/HSPs seem to be very emotionally intense individuals with self-care being of critical importance to their long-term health. For these individuals there must be a balance between high sensation-seeking and high sensitivity. The need to apply a high degree of mindfulness seems especially important to HSS/HSPs. High sensation-seeking HSPs may find having a career to be problematic, especially with regards to boredom and burnout. The best compromise seems to be cultivating an orientation toward life that indulges the high sensation-seeking side, while respecting the needs of the highly sensitive side. For HSS/HSPs this may mean they are not well-suited to a conventional definition of career. Jung (1913) described those with innate sensitiveness to be on a highly individual path, here it seems to apply more so. For HSS/HSPs finding the right balance between an optimal level of stimulation and overstimulation is paramount. The implications of driven creativity, however seem to justify seeking such a balance.

HSS/HSPs seek novelty, new experiences, and are highly creative. Employers may find these individuals to be the most emotionally intense and driven, but are also susceptible to burnout if their need for self-care is not adequately addressed. Employers should make the extra effort to develop these individual's potential, yet avoid overloading them. They may potentially be the most creative, most innovative employees if handled with care. HSS/HSPs should know themselves well; seek to find and maintain a balance between the need to seek new sensation and the need to recharge and rest; and be willing to forgive themselves gently for overstepping their own boundaries. HSS/HSPs need to practice self-care diligently and engage in their choice of spiritual practices mindful of their own intensity and novelty-seeking tendencies.

Self Determination Theory's emphasis (Deci & Ryan, 2000) on intrinsic needs seems to apply to all HSPs. However, HSS/HSPs appear to have deeper needs for an alignment between external demands and their internal capabilities with the additional requirement of limited duration projects. In my search of the existing literature I was not able to locate anything related to this finding. I suggest that for HSS/HSPs attending to their basic psychological needs, as outlined in SDT, carries with it a greater psychological "penalty" if these needs are not met. HSS/HSPs in unsatisfactory situations may be more likely than HSPs to feel they need to leave a position.

Discussion of Results for Theme 7: The Sociological Perspective

Results from this umbrella theme illustrate the picture of complexity that emerged from this study. Separated into culture, social class, race, and gender sub-themes the results from each indicate significant differences in the way HSPs experience careers. First, cultural differences were included in this study to better inform the overall understanding. Though only five foreign countries are represented in this study the results add to the dimension and depth of explication of SPS. Based on the descriptions of participants it seems the greatest level of awareness of SPS exists in the U.S. The overall level of understanding and acceptance of SPS in other cultures in this study seems to be low. Chouko related that in Japan there is almost no awareness of SPS and it is often confused or attributed to neuroticism or shyness. Japan is known to be an introverted culture where one might expect HSPs to be better understood or accepted, but, according to Chouko SPS is not known and while HSPs may find the culture more suitable overall there is still no understanding of the trait.

Chouko related that many of the books written to date about SPS have not been translated into Japanese.

Ning reported that Chinese culture is rooted in meditation, thus Chinese HSPs may have a stronger, built-in spiritual practice that does not exist in the U.S. Chinese culture is less focused on the individual and more on the group. As a communally-oriented culture Chinese HSPs may not realize they are HSPs due to this overall focus on others. The strong, meditative emphasis may also place Chinese HSPs at an advantage preventing overstimulation to the degree HSPs in the U.S. experience.

Ning and Chouko's respective cultural emphasis on concern for others, meditation, and introversion as the norm may make life as a HSP easier in the sense that the majority of people value introspection and a deep inner life, however the specific needs of HSPs may go unnoticed, unacknowledged, or unappreciated. HSPs in this situation may find this to be a frustrating life, but more research would need to be conducted to better understand HSPs in China or Japan. I feel there is great promise in incorporating Eastern meditative and religious practices for HSPs in the U.S. With centuries of experience in the "inner life" it seems Western culture could benefit greatly from integrating Eastern practices, but done in a way that honors and respects existing cultural practices.

Vitaly reported no specific details distinguishing Russia as a country that is more accepting or understanding if SPS. His descriptions centered on the clash of gender role expectations with males in Russia subscribing to a traditional hegemonic view of masculinity. In that sense, to be a male HSP in Russia could potentially be very problematic due to the non-inclusive nature of the culture. Astrid reported a less confrontational attitude toward HSPs in Denmark, but stated there is no understanding of SPS there.

Awareness and appreciation of SPS seems to be highest in the U.S. at present. This is likely due to most of the research connected to SPS having been carried out in the U.S. As books and other media are translated into other languages it may be likely that awareness increases over time, however acceptance of SPS may be some time in coming due to cultural lag.

Social class was expected to exert significant influence on how HSPs experience careers. As mentioned in chapter four the majority of participants in this study possess post-secondary education, thus the lower and upper classes are not proportionately represented, though many of the participants started life under humble circumstances. The responses in this study seem to indicate that participants may begin their lives attempting to fulfill the expectations of others, but their sensitive natures tend to limit their ability to fully carry that out. Many reported arriving at a point in life where they realized they could no longer live to fulfill the wishes of others, instead coming to a profound awakening oriented toward personal authenticity. This may involve a complete divestiture of cultural conditioning specific to each social class, but it is likely a significant portion of social class tendencies remain. Participants did report steps they have taken to ensure their children, who are often also HSPs, have a better childhood and school experience than they did. This seems to acknowledge failings in their own backgrounds that served to impede their ability to live with personal authenticity. Social class also seems to play an important role in acceptance of SPS, especially during childhood. The lower social classes tend to not emphasize creativity, sensitivity, or originality instead favoring conformity, obedience, and instrumental traits necessary for economic survival (Bowles & Gintis, 1976, 2002). The emphasis is on reproducing the existing social class structure with parents assuming their children will likely work in jobs similar to theirs, rather than on developing individuals to their maximum potential. Traditional views regarding one's "place" in the world seems to have been problematic for many of the participants.

For HSPs from higher socioeconomic classes there may be more of an acceptance and appreciation for creative, sensitive individuals based on the perception that the types of careers their children will work in will require more creativity and offer more autonomy for this type of work. Children from middle class families are also likely to be afforded opportunities for greater development of creative capacities through camps and workshops that enhance and strengthen creative skills and abilities. HSPs from supportive, nurturing backgrounds of this type may be more likely to be accepted for exhibiting sensitivity.

The sociological principle most clearly related to many of the HSPs in this study, beyond social class, is status inconsistency (Lenski, 1954; 1966; Dogan, 2011). Individuals who are status inconsistent may occupy a higher social status in one sense, yet experience a lower status in reality. As noted previously the majority of participants in this study possess at least a bachelor's degree. For those who have achieved an advanced education having to move from position to position in search of one that satisfies an individual's intrinsic needs may produce a strong sense of occupying a higher social status in terms of prestige and respect, while working in a lesser position to accommodate their actual needs as HSPs. Though status inconsistency is not a dominant theme in this study it is relevant to the experience of approximately one-third of the participants.

Of the three major sociological theories: conflict theory, functionalism, and symbolic interactionism, the one that seems most pertinent to this study is conflict theory (Marx & Engels, 1967). Conflict theory predominantly considers struggles for power based on controlling means of production or other means that provide one power over others, but in this case the struggle of participants in this study is not for an equality of power. Rather, it seems to be more of a struggle to gain power over one's life, including interpersonal and physical working conditions with the added moral component of doing work that adheres to ethical standards. Dabrowski's TPD seems to intertwine well with this struggle for personal power as it exemplifies the strong drive many participants reported to live in ways that are authentic to their intrinsic needs.

This study did not directly address the role of race in the experience of careers, however it is likely the implications are crucial to an in-depth understanding of HSPs in the workplace. Guy related that his experience of race has seemingly been more important, or at least as important, as his experience of SPS. His accounts of having to utilize empathy in a self-protective way stood in contrast to the other participants. Guy's background of privilege also may represent an atypical experience for African-American HSPs.

The findings on gender in this study represent one of the major differences in the way HSPs experience careers with male HSPs encountering the additional burden of clashes with the hegemonic view of masculinity to which most families in the U.S. still subscribe. The descriptions of unacceptance of sensitivity by fathers reinforced this view. From the responses of the male participants, I surmised a sense of androgyny seemed to replace hegemonic masculinity as the preferred trait expression. Seth especially seemed to embody a confident expression of healthy androgyny based in what he described as being secure within himself to express both instrumental and expressive traits.

The male participants reported conflicts with others over gender role expectations and seem to have learned to "hide away" their sensitivity to conform to social norms. Embodying a secure form of masculinity that encompasses instrumental and expressive traits (androgyny) appears to hold the greatest promise for male HSPs (Zeff, 2010). In the workplace males may find more acceptance of SPS depending on the nature of their work. Males in professional positions may find that expressive traits are valued, particularly where cooperation, mentoring, and personal caring are involved. Males in helping professions may be at the greatest advantage with regards to acceptance of SPS. Though the number of male HSPs in this study was statistically small the findings seem to correlate with Zeff's (2010) observations about highly sensitive males.

Discussion of Results for Theme 8: The Experience of Work

This study was designed to better understand how HSPs experience careers. In order to develop a deep appreciation of the many variables it was necessary to examine the way HSPs experience life from relevant perspectives. Chapter four contained themes detailing the internal and external experiences of HSPs. This theme combines together all the previous ones focusing strictly on the experience of work. My data analysis led to the consideration of a number of pertinent elements. Interpersonal relationships factored prominently in this analysis. HSPs reported varying social preferences from significant introversion and a need for low sociability to extraversion and a need for high sociability. Most reported expression of both traits at different times as expedient, thus more introverted HSPs can become extraverted to deal with customers or interact with other necessary personnel. A need for a period of quiet time to recharge was expressed by all participants regardless of social preference.

The role of positive feedback, specifically the need expressed by many HSPs to receive positive feedback or affirmation is a repetitive theme in this study. Many HSPs reported not receiving positive feedback or affirmations. As previously noted HSPs process positive energy more deeply than others and tend to do better than average when they receive it. The lack of positive energy in the workplace may be detrimental to long-term satisfaction in a position for HSPs. Though it is not always possible to arrange work where one has a supervisor that provides positive feedback or practices positive leadership it seems highly advisable for HSPs to seek such employment. A positive work environment also needs to be harmonious. The HSPs in this study reported a strong dislike for workplace conflict and for superficiality. Both may contribute to boredom and burnout leading to the HSP leaving a position.

The physical environment of work includes everything in the built environment and for HSPs seems to be mostly sensory in nature. Environmental attributes that are undermining to HSPs therefore, include bright lights; strong smells; fluctuations of temperature; crowded office spaces; distracting noises; and disorder. Though any of these issues might bother anyone, HSPs seem to be more deeply affected than others and may make significant concessions in order to attain a socially communicated view of success. Other HSPs may choose to risk long-term career viability and success in favor of more personally appropriate working situations with less environmental distractions. The sensory environment for HSPs may prove intolerable and employers may feel no obligation to change what may work for the bulk of its workforce, placing HSPs at a disadvantage in such situations. HSPs who choose to remain in continuously overstimulating environments may learn to numb themselves to an extent, possibly entering a state of alienation to avoid the need to process overstimulation. In such cases the importance of self-care becomes of even greater importance.

HSPs in this study related a strong need for

autonomy. Many reported a dislike for being watched while working or feeling as if they were being watched. Most also expressed a strong need for time and space to think while they focus on the task. As previously noted the rich inner life of HSPs is one of contemplation, introspection, and complexity. The need for autonomy, and time and space to think mirror the conditions one would expect from a complex individual. Participants seem to struggle with being able to have their needs met at work. Many described workplaces that simply demand conformity and offer little in the way of flexibility. If HSPs serve the role of vanguard for the human species what is being expressed is a need for more humane workplaces where introspective individuals are afforded the freedom to fulfill their potential.

The need for meaningful work was strongly expressed by participants. This seems to support the contentions of self-determination theory that intrinsic needs of the individual are viewed as more valuable than extrinsic needs. Similarly SDT's conceptualization of basic psychological needs fulfillment seems to be supported in this study. Beyond these basic contentions the participants in this study, by virtue of their expressed conscientiousness, seem to have articulated a vision for a more authentic way of being that includes authentic work or work that is aligned with personal needs and beliefs on intellectual, spiritual, and creative levels.

Dabrowski's (1964) theory of positive disintegration seems to offer a useful lens through which the fundamental dispositional elements that comprise many HSPs personalities can be viewed. Dabrowski's theory is one of personal development and growth with individuals high in certain overexcitabilities possessing what he termed developmental potential. Overexcitabilities, by Dabrowski's definition, includes sensory, intellectual, emotional, psychomotor, and sensual aspects: (see Chapter 2, "Alternate Conceptions" of the current study). In TPD those individuals who possess emotional, intellectual, and imaginational overexcitabilities may have the greatest developmental potential. He felt those individuals high in developmental potential would possess a strong drive toward personal autonomy. Progressing through a series of levels a person high in developmental potential will undergo a series of personal "disintegrations," usually brought on by crises, where one's ideas, beliefs, values, and thoughts reintegrate in a new configuration oriented toward higher, more altruistic values and goals (Dabrowski, 1972). Not all individuals with heightened sensitivities will undergo positive disintegration, according to TPD, but many of the participants in this study appear to possess high developmental potential and be on the highly individualized path of TPD.

Discussion of Results for Theme 9: The Integral Being

The last theme in this study synthesizes the aforementioned desire for a more personally authentic way of being in the world as expressed by participants. Integral being is metaphorical for a more inclusive, holistic way of being that enables and encourages realization of one's full potential, while simultaneously identifying such a person. *Integral being* is a verb and a noun. Participants in this study cumulatively expressed their journeys of self-discovery; finding acceptance of their sensitivity; and learning to thrive. Descriptions of radical self-acceptance; forgiveness of self; and being totally awake seemed to indicate an expressed desire for a form of transcendence. The HSPs in this study exhibited introspection; contemplativeness; gregariousness; openness; humility; strength; perseverance; resilience; defeat; joy; creativity in thought and action; immense caring for others; and a desire to live as integral beings.

The implications for those who achieve this state of being are enormous for society. Kirk articulated it this way,

> I discovered that I was not immortal...I just realized that, ok, I don't have unlimited time. That just changed my whole perspective of what mattered to me or what was important. I went through a year or two after that where I just didn't even know if I wanted to be here anymore, because it was so miserable in my job. I guess what I am trying to get to, is I sort of reason down my life in terms of its priority on the basis of at the moment of my death how am I going to see this? Am I going to feel like I was everything I could be, as authentic as I can be to the best of my ability or am I going to feel like I was just kind of making sacrifices to fit in with other people and do what they want?

The pressures of time and mortality weigh on all of us, but perhaps more strongly on HSPs. The participants in this study expressed their fervent desire to live their authentic selves, to fulfill their potential, and to serve a larger purpose.

TPD, as mentioned in the previous discussion, offers a way of viewing the inherent potentialities of HSPs with a greater emphasis on a model of how development occurs for individuals high in developmental potential.

On another level, examining HSPs from a Western mindset may limit the conclusions of this study because of the tendency to weigh the facts and find solutions. In the larger context HSPs have always been a part of the human saga. The integral being likely serves a function in the survival of the species; it is only in the present where we have created an economic structure that exhibits a decided preference for extraverted, aggressive, and competitive personalities that we risk excluding those of a different temperament.

Future Research

The implications of this study are far-reaching with numerous future research possibilities. In this section I will present some of the major directions future research could investigate.

The role of empathy in the workplace including the moral issues associated with possible manipulation or exploitation represents a major area that needs more exploration. More work to help HSPs better understand how to manage the continual absorption of the energy of others seems advisable. I suggest a Taoist-inspired viewpoint that accepts "what is," while encouraging mindful practices. Researchers could explore ways of managing empathy while respecting its inherent potentialities.

Future research could address HSPs and giftedness

with a special emphasis on the expectations of others and of self. Research could also be carried out on the early childhood needs of HSPs in order to better ascertain more appropriate parental methods for early childhood. Additional research could investigate the way the school environment influences HSPs' development.

Researchers could explore the needs of creative HSPs. Understanding the conditions that make optimal creativity possible for HSPs would facilitate innovation and imaginative new products, services, and corporate orientations. Other research could explore what it means to be a creative HSP, how it affects the overall life course, and how creativity can be balanced with other capacities in a holistic way. The cosmological motive Barron (1995) described could be explored as HSPs utilize their creativity to forge lives based on the aforementioned deep motivation or drive to create. Barron's aforementioned cosmological motive seems to be very similar to Dabrowski's (1964) "third factor." These two concepts should be compared and contrasted to determine if they are synonymous conceptualizations. Similarly, Dabrowski's (1964) TPD should be more fully examined to better understand how it applies to HSPs on many levels of development. I am particularly interested in the TPD applies to HSS/HSPs because they seemed to possess the strongest drive toward personality development.

Research could explore the lives of HSS/HSPs and distinguish how they differ from HSPs. Research also needs to determine the percentage of HSS/HSPs. Well-researched instruments need to be devised and tested for this purpose.

Creativity seems to be extremely strong in HSS/HSPs. Future research could determine the types of creative endeavors HSPs are engaged in to better understand the lives and propensities of HSPs.

Researchers could explore numerous aspects of male HSPs including better understanding of what it means to be a male HSP in a non-accepting culture; investigating our own bias rooted in our Eurocentric viewpoint which may prove to be too limiting; how to embody an integral masculinity that expresses a balanced androgyny; and how to develop and implement more appropriate parenting techniques that honor and respect HSP males as children. Additional research could explore the experience of male HSPs in school and healing from accumulated trauma. The latter particularly seems pertinent given the extent to which male HSPs seem to experience rejection.

Further research could explore why employer resistance exists with regards to creativity; the role of HSPs in the workplace; and pedagogies designed to enhance workplace design and harmony. Future research could explore the conditions under which a HSP feels an alignment between intrinsic motivations and extrinsic has occurred; more specific work relating SDT to HSPs; and the implications of authentic work for our society. Lastly, future research could look at SPS from an evolutionary standpoint in an attempt to better understand the role HSPs have played in the past as "canaries in the coal mine" and possibly inform a future where integral being is not just for HSPs, but for everyone as workplaces continue to evolve and change in response to needs to remain competitive in the global marketplace. If HSPs serve a function as the vanguard of human sensitivity what affects HSPs may eventually affect the general population. The challenge may be to rediscover our inner lives and the gifts we all hold inside.

Limitations

This study elucidated a broad range of variables for further study, but was limited by the sample size. Further study utilizing the variables identified could be performed to determine generalizability across the HSP population. This would take the form of a quantitative survey perhaps with questions derived from the nine themes. A further limitation exists with regards to the interview format. Though I feel the participants provided the best responses they were capable of any attempt at encapsulating complex experiences is elusive. Interviewing individuals who are non-HSPs might provide a basis for comparison. The themes identified in this study are emergent and exploratory. With further data the themes would undoubtedly continue to transform with layers of new meaning and context. A study of this nature can only hope to provide a better understanding that opens the door to additional study. In that regard I feel this study has accomplished its goals of providing a better understanding of how HSPs experience careers.

Conclusion

This study attempted to understand the complex nature of how HSPs experience careers. Nine distinct themes emerged from the data analysis, which elucidated a complex reality for HSPs in the workplace. Major findings of this study suggest that HSPs high in empathy experience the greatest challenge to managing the energy absorbed from others; HSPs who experienced difficult childhoods may do better than expected if they are able to overcome or mitigate lingering emotional issues; self-care is crucial for HSPs to function at optimal levels sustainably with the additional importance of a strong spiritual practice; male HSPs experience the extra burden of hegemonic masculinity expectations; approximately 90 percent of HSPs in this study seemed to fit a complex definition of creativity; approximately one-third of HSPs in this study are high sensation-seeking HSPs; the experience of work is complex with significant interpersonal ramifications; and the desire to pursue authentic work drives the HSPs in this study toward a fuller integration of all the traits they possess. The findings in this study are tentative, emergent and suggest the need for further research to more fully explore the extent to which the variables identified apply to the broader HSP population and, by extension, to the general population.

I undertook this study in an attempt to know myself better, to generate new knowledge with the potential of alleviating suffering, and to increase the capacity of HSPs to navigate the complex nature of careers. In a personal sense it has been illuminating and gratifying to finally understand that "there is nothing wrong with me." In another sense the journey continues because more research is needed to inform the emerging image of the integral being provided here. Undertaking a journey such as this entails a certain amount of personal risk as new perspectives and experiences are related that potentially contribute to dissolution of self.

Here is where the value of Dabrowski's TPD seems to play an especially important role in the growth process informing and influencing a reconstituted self. The period of cocooning that Slater (2009) spoke of dissolved old views I held and, after a period of incubation, a transformation did occur and I emerged bearing knowledge to share with all as we travel the roads of self-discovery, self-acceptance, and progress toward an integral being.

References

Acevedo, B., Aron, A., Aron, E., Sangster, M., Collins, N., & Brown, L. (2014). The highly sensitive brain: An fMRI study of sensory processing sensitivity and response to others' emotions. *Brain and Behavior, 4*, 1-15.

Alarcon, G., Eschleman, K., & Bowling, N. (2009). Relationships between personality variables and burnout: A meta-analysis. *Work and Stress, 23*(3), 244-263.

Allport, G., & Odbert, H. (1936). Trait-names: a psycho-lexical study. *Psychological Monographs, 47*(1), 1-36.

Anderson, C., John, O., Keltner, D., & Kring, A. (2001). Who attains social status? Effects Of personality and physical attractiveness in social groups. *Journal of Personality and Social Psychology, 81,* 116-132.

Anderson, C., & Kilduff, G. (2009). Why do dominant personalities attaininfluence in face-to-face groups? The competence-signaling effects of trait dominance. *Journal of Personality and Social Psychology, 96*(2), 491-503.

Arkin, R. (1981). *Self-presentation styles. Impression management theory andsocial psychological research.* New York, NY: Academic Press.

Aron, A., & Aron, E. (1997). Sensory-processing sensitivity and its relation to introversion and emotionality. *Journal of Personality and Social Psychology, 73*, 345-368.

Aron, A., Aron., E., & Jagiellowicz, J. (2012). Sensory processing sensitivity: A review in the light of the evolution of biological responsivity. *Personality and Social Psychology Review, 16*, 262-282.

Aron, E. (2006). The clinical implications Jung's concept of sensitiveness.   *Journal of Jungian Theory and Practice, 8*(2), 11-43.

Aron, E. (2000). *The highly sensitive person in love*. New York, NY: Broadway Books.

Aron, E. (2010). *Psychotherapy and the highly sensitive person: Improving outcomes for that minority of people who are the majority of clients*. New York, NY: Routledge.

Aron, E., Aron, A., & Davies, K. (2005). Adult shyness: The interaction of temperamental sensitivity and an adverse childhood environment. *Personality and Social Psychology Bulletin, 31*, 181-197.

Barrick, M., & Mount, M. (2003). Impact of meta-analysis methods on understanding personality–performance relations. In K. Murphy (Ed.), *Validity generalization: A critical review* (pp. 197–222). Mahwah, NJ: Lawrence Erlbaum.

Barrick, M., & Mount, M. (1991). The Big Five personality dimensions and job performance: A meta-analysis. *Personnel Psychology, 44*(1), 1–26.

Barrick, M., & Mount, M. (2003). Impact of meta-analysis methods on understanding personality–performance relations. In K. Murphy (Ed.), *Validity generalization: A critical review* (pp. 197–222). Mahwah, NJ: Lawrence Erlbaum.

Barrick, M., Stewart, G., & Mount, M. (1998). Relating member ability and personality to work-team processes and team effectiveness. *Journal of Applied Psychology, 83*(3), 377–391.

Barron, F. (1995). *No rootless flower.* Cresskill, NJ: Hampton Press.

Barry, B., & Stewart, G. (1997). Composition, process, and performance in self-managed groups: The role of personality. *Journal of Applied Psychology, 82*(1), 62-78.

Baumeister, F., Vohs, D., DeWall, N., & Zhang, L. (2007). How emotion shapes behavior: feedback, anticipation, and reflection, rather than direct causation. *Personality and Social Psychology Review, 11,* 167-203.

Baumgarten, F. (1933). The character traits. *Beitraege zur Charakter und Persoenlichkeitsforschung, 1*(3), 15-22.

Beagrie, S. (2005). How to excel at psychometric assessments. *Personnel Today, 25.* Retrieved from http://www.personneltoday.com/articles/2005/03/22/28745/ psychometrics-how-to-excel-at-psychometric-assessments.html.

Bem, S. (1974). The measurement of psychological androgyny. *Journal of Consulting and Clinical Psychology, 42*, 155-162.

Bendersky, C., & Shah, N. (2013). The costs of status attainment: Performance effects of individual's status mobility in task groups. *Organization Science, 23*(2), 308-322.

Biernacki, P., & Waldorf, D. (1981). Snowball sampling: Problems and techniques of chain referral sampling. *Sociological Methods & Research,* 32, 148–170

Block, J. (1995). A contrarian view of the five-factor approach to personality description. *Psychological Bulletin, 117*(2), 187–215.

Bowles, S., & Gintis, H. (1976). *Schooling in capitalistic America.* New York, NY: Basic Books.

Bowles, S., & Gintis, H. (2002). Schooling in capitalistic America revisited. *Sociology of Education, 75*, 1-18.

Brandstatter, H., & Eliaz, A. (2001). *Person, situations, and emotions: An ecological approach.* New York, NY: Oxford University Press.

Broeck, A., Vansteenkiste, M., De Witte, H., Soenens, B., & Lens, W. (2010). Capturing autonomy, competence, and relatedness at work: Construction and initial validation of the work-related Basic Need Satisfaction scale. *Journal of Occupational and Organizational Psychology, 83*(4), 981-1002.

Campbell, J. (1971). *The portable Jung*. New York, NY: The Viking Press.

Cattell, R. (1943). The description of personality: Basic traits resolved into clusters. *Journal of Abnormal and Social Psychology, 38*(4), 476-506.

Cattell, R. (1945a). The description of personality: Principles and findings in a factor analysis. *American Journal of Psychology, 58,* 69-90.

Cattell, R. (1945b). The principal trait clusters for describing personality. *Psychological   Bulletin, 42,* 129-161.

Chaplain, W., John, O., & Goldberg, L. (1988). Conceptions of states and traits: dimensional attributes with ideals as prototypes. *Journal of Personality and Social Psychology, 54*(4), 541-557.

Cloninger, C. (1987). A systematic method for clinical description and classification of personality variants: A proposal. *Archives of General Psychiatry, 44*(6), 573-588.

Connell, R. (1995). *Masculinities*. Berkley, CA: University of California Press.

Costa, P., & McCrae, R. (1985). *The NEO personality inventory manual*. Odessa, FL: Psychological Assessment Resources.

Costa, P., & McCrae, R. (1992). *NEO-R professional manual*. Odessa, FL: Psychological Assessment Resources.

Costa, P., & McCrae, R. (1993). Bullish on personality psychology. *The Psychologist, 6*, 302-303.

Costa, P., & McCrae, R. (1998). Six approaches to the explication of facet-level traits: examples from conscientiousness. *European Journal of Personality, 12*, 117-134. Retrieved from http://subjectpool.com/ed_teach/y4person/2_facets/refs/Costa_1998_uses_of_facets.pdf.

Creswell, J. (2003). *Research design: Qualitative, quantitative, and mixed methods approaches*. Thousand Oaks, CA: Sage.

Csikszentmihalyi, M. (1975). *Beyond boredom and anxiety*. San Francisco: Jossey-Bass Ltd.

Csikszentmihalyi, M. (1992a). *Flow: The psychology of happiness*. London: Harper and Row.

Csikszentmihalyi, M. (1992b). The measurement of flow in everyday life: Toward a theory of emergent motivation. In J. Jacobs (Ed.). *Nebraska Symposium on Motivation,* 40, 57-97.

Csikszentmihalyi, M. (1996). *Creativity: Flow and the psychology of discovery and invention.* New York, NY: HarperCollins Publisher.

Dabrowski, K. (1964). *Positive disintegration.* London: Little Brown.

Dabrowski, K. (1967). *Personality shaping through positive disintegration.* Boston, MA: Little Brown.

Dabrowski, K. (1972). *Psychoneurosis is not an illness.* London: Gryf Publications.

Dabrowski, K. & Piechowski, M. (1970). *Mental Growth Through Positive Disintegration.* London: Gryf Publications LTD.

David, D., & Brannon, R. (1976). *The forty-nine percent majority: The male sex role.* Reading, MA: Addison-Wesley.

Deci, E. & Ryan, R. (2000). The "what" and "why" of goal pursuits: Human needs and the self-determination of behavior. *Psychological Inquiry, 11*(4), 227-268.

Dogan, M. (2011). Status incongruence in advanced societies. *Societamutamentopolitica, 2*(3), 285-294.

Donaldson, M. (1993). What is hegemonic masculinity? *Theory and*

Society, 22(5), 643-657

Eisenberg, N., Fabes, R., Guthrie, I., & Reiser, M. (2002). The role of emotionality and regulation in children's social competence and adjustment. In L. Pulkkinen (Ed.), *Paths to successful development: Personality in the life course* (pp. 46-72). West Nyack, NY: Cambridge Press

Erickson, P. (2004, May 16). Employer hiring tests grow sophisticated in quest for insight about applicants. *Knight Ridder Tribune Business News,* p.1.

Elliot, A., & Thrash, T. (2002). Approach-avoidance motivation in personality: Approach and avoidance temperaments and goals. *Journal of Personality and Social Psychology, 82,* 804-818

Eysenck, H. (1957). *The dynamics of anxiety and hysteria.* New York, NY: Praeger.

Eysenck, H. (1981*). A model for personality.* New York, NY: Springer-Verlag.

Eysenck, H. (1991). Dimensions of personality: 16, 5, or 3? Criteria for a taxonomy paradigm. *Personality and Individual Differences, 12*(8), 773–790.

Evers, A., Rasche, J., & Schabracq, M. (2008). High sensory-processing sensitivity at work. *International Journal of Stress*

Management, 15(2), 189-198.

Falk, R., Manzanero, J., & Miller, N. (1997). Developmental potential in Venezuelan and American artists: A cross cultural validity study. *Creativity Journal, 10*, 201-206.

Fernet, C., Gagné, M., & Austin, S. (2010). When does quality of relationships with coworkers predict burnout over time? The moderating role of work motivation. *Journal of Organizational Behavior, 31*, 1163-1180.

Fine, B. (1972). Field-dependent introvert and neuroticism: Eysenck and Witkin united. *Psychological Reports, 31,* 939-956.

Fine, B. (1973). Field-dependence-independence as "sensitivity" of the nervous system: Supportive evidence with color and weight discrimination. *Perceptual and Motor Skills, 37,* 287-295.

Fiske, D. (1949). Consistency of the factorial structures of personality ratings from different sources. *Journal of Abnormal and Social Psychology, 44,* 329-344.

Frankl, V. (1984). *Man's search for meaning.* New York, NY: Simon and Schuster, Inc.

Goldberg, L. (1981). Language and individual differences: the search for universals in personality lexicons. In L. Wheeler (Ed.), *Review of Personality and Social Psychology, 2*, 141-165.

Goldberg, L. (1990). An alternative description of personality: The Big Five factor structure. *Journal of Personality and Social Psychology, 59*, 1216-1229.

Goldberg, L., & Saucier, G. (1996). Evidence for the Big Five in analyses of familiar English personality adjectives. *European Journal of Personality, 10*, 61-77. Retrieved from http://pages.uoregon.edu/prsnlty/SAUCIER/Saucier_1996_EJP.pdf

Gray, J. (1981). A critique of Eysenck's theory of personality. In H. Eysenck (Ed.), *A model for personality* (pp. 246-276). New York, NY: Springer.

Gray, J. (1985). Issues in the neuropsychology of anxiety. In A. Tuma, J. Maser (Eds.), *Anxiety and disorder* (pp. 5-25). Hillsdale, NJ: Erlbaum.

Gray, J. (1991). The neurophysiology of temperament. In J. Strelau, A. Angleitner (Eds.), *Explorations in temperament: International perspectives on theory and measurement,* (pp. 105-128). New York, NY: Plenum.

Groothuis, T. & Carere, C. (2005). Avian personalities: Characterization and epigenesis. *Neuroscience and Biobehavioral Reviews, 29*(2), 137-150.

Gunnar, M.R. (1994). Psychoendocrine studies of temperament and stress in early childhood: Expanding current models. In J. Bates & T. Wachs (Eds.), *Temperament: Individual differences at the interface of biology and behavior* (pp. 175-198). Washington, DC: American Psychological Association.

Hartmann, E. (1992). *Boundaries in the mind: A new psychology of personality.* New York, NY: Harper-Collins.

Hartmann, E. (2011). *Boundaries: A new way to look at the world.* Summerland, CA: CIRCC Everpress.

Heller, M. (2005). Court ruling that employer's integrity test violated ADA could open door to litigation. *Workforce Management, 84*(9), 74–77.

Higgins, T. (2000). Making a good decision: Value from fit. *American Psychologist, 55*, 1217-1230.

Hogan, R. (1986). *Hogan personality inventory manual.* Minneapolis, MN: National Computer Systems.

Hogan, R., & Hogan, J. (1991). Personality and status. In D. Gilbert, & J. Connolly (Eds.), *Personality, social skills and psychopathology An individual differences approach*: (pp.137 –154). New York: Plenum Press.

Hogan, R., Johnson, J., & Briggs, S. (1997). *Handbook of personality psychology.* San Diego, CA: Academic Press.

Hough, L. (1992). The "Big Five" personality variables–construct confusion: description versus prediction. *Human Performance, 5*(1), 139–155.

Hough, L. (1998a). Effects of intentional distortion in personality measurement and evaluation of suggested palliatives. *Human Performance, 11*, 209–244. Retrieved from http://www.tandfonline.com/doi/abs/10.1080/08959285.1998.9668032 .

Hough, L. (1998b). Personality at work: Issues and evidence. In M. Hakel (Ed.), *Beyond multiple choice: Evaluating alternatives to traditional testing for selection* (pp. 131–166). Mahwah, NJ: Lawrence Erlbaum Associates.

Izard, C., & Ackerman, B. (2000). Motivation, organizational, and regulatory functions of discrete emotions. In M. Lewis & J. Heviland-Jones (Eds.), *Handbook of emotions* (2nd ed., pp. 253-264). New York, NY: Guilford.

Jackson, D. (1984). *Personality research form manual* (3rd ed.). Port Huron, MI: Research Psychologists.

Jaeger, B. (2004). *Making work work for the highly sensitive person.* New York, NY: McGraw-Hill.

John, O. & Srivastava, S. (1999). The Big Five trait taxonomy:

History, measurement, and theoretical perspectives. In O. John & L. Pervin (Eds.), *Handbook of personality* (pp. 102-138). New York, NY: The Guilford Press.

Judge, T., Higgins, C., Thoresen, C., & Barrick, M. (1999). The big five personality traits, general mental ability, and career success across the life span. *Personnel Psychology, 52*(3), 621-652.

Jung, C. (1913). *The theory of psychoanalysis*. Collected Works, Vol. 4. Princeton, NJ: The Princeton University Press.

Jung, C. (1921). *Psychological types*. Collected Works, Vol. 6. Princeton, NJ: The Princeton University Press.

Kagan, J. (1994). *Galen's prophecy: Temperament in human nature.* New York, NY: Basic Books.

Kimmel, M. & Kaufman, M. (1994). *Weekend warriors: The new men's movement.* Thousand Oaks, CA: Sage.

Klages, L. (1926). *The science of character*. London, England: George Allen and Unwin.

Koolhaas, J., Korte, S., De Boer, S., Van Der Vegt, B., Van Reenen, C., Hopster, H., et al. (1999). Coping styles in animals: Current status in behavior and stress physiology. *Neuroscience and Biobehavioral Reviews, 23*(7), 925-935.

Leavy, P. (2011). *Essentials of transdisciplinary research*. Walnut Creek, CA: Left Coast Press.

Lensky, G. (1954). Status crystallization: A nonverticle dimension of social status. *American Sociological Review, 19*(4), 405-413.

Lensky, G. (1966). *Power and privilege: A theory of social stratification*. New York, NY: McGraw-Hill.

Lincoln, Y., & Guba, E. (1985). *Naturalistic inquiry*. Newbury Park, CA: SAGE Publications, Inc.

Markus, H., & Nurius, P. (1986). Possible selves. *American Psychologist, 41*(9), 954-969.

Marx, K., and Engles, F. (1967). *Communist manifesto*. New York, NY: Pantheon.

Martanuska, J. (2012). "The princess and the pea:" Suggestions for the revision of sensory sensitivity in the regulative theory of temperament. *Journal of Individual Differences, 33*(4), 237-247.

Martin, M., Sadlo, G., & Stew, G. (2006). The phenomenon of boredom. *Qualitative Research in Psychology, 3*(3), 193-211.

Maslow A. (1968). *Toward a psychology of being*. New York, NY: D Van Nostrand Company.

Maxwell, J. (2005). *Qualitative research design: An interactive approach*. Thousand Oaks, CA: Sage.

McNaughton, N., & Gray, J. (2000). Anxiolytic action on the behavioural inhibition system implies multiple types of arousal contribute to anxiety. *Journal of Affective Disorders, 61*(3), 161-176.

McRae, R., & John, O. (1992). An introduction to the five-factor model and its applications. *Journal of Personality*, 60, 175-215.

McCrae, R. (1992). The five-factor model: issues and applications. (Special Issue) *Journal of Personality, 60*.

McCrae, R., & Costa, P. (1999). Age differences in personality across the lifespan: parallels in five cultures. *Developmental Psychology, 35*, 466-477.

Mednick, S. (1962). The associative basis of the creative process. *Psychological   Review, 69*, 220-232.

Mehrabian, A. (1976*). Manual for the questionnaire measure of stimulus screening and arousability*. (Unpublished manuscript.) University of California, Los Angeles.

Mehrabian, A. (1991). Outline of a general emotion-based theory of temperament. In J. Strelan & A. Angleitner (Eds*.), Explorations in temperament: International perspectives on theory and measurement* (pp. 75-86). New York: Plenum.

Mehrabian, A., & O'Reilly, E. (1980). Analysis of personality measures in terms of basic dimensions of temperament. *Journal of Personality and Social Psychology, 38*(3), 492-503.

Mendaglio, S. (2008). *Dabrowski's theory of positive disintegration.* Scottsdale, AR: Great Potential Press, Inc.

Mills, C. (1959) *The sociological imagination.* New York, NY: Oxford University Press.

Montuori, A. (2008). The joy of inquiry. *Journal of Transformative Education, 6*(1), 8-26.

Norman, W. (1967). *Two thousand eight hundred personality trait descriptors: Normative operating characteristics for a university population.* Department of Psychology, University of Michigan, Ann Arbor, MI .Retrieved from http://files.eric.ed.gov/fulltext/ED014738.pdf

O'Neil, J. (1981). Patterns of gender role conflict and strain: Sexism and fear of femininity in men's lives. *The Personnel and Guidance Journal, 60*(4), 203-210.

Patterson, C., & Newman, J. (1993). Reflectivity and learning from aversive events: Toward a psychological mechanism for the syndromes of disinhibition. *Psychological Review, 100*(4), 716-736.

Pleck, J. (1981). *The myth of masculinity*. Cambridge, MA: MIT Press.

Rome, D., & Martin, H. (2010). Are you listening? *Shambhala Sun, 18*, 56-60.

Rothstein, M., & Goffin, R. (2006). The use of personality measures in personnel selection: what does current research support? *Human Resource Management Review, 16*(2), 155-180.

Rubin, H., and Rubin, I. (1995). *Qualitative interviewing: The art of hearing data*. Thousand Oaks, CA: SAGE Publications, Inc.

Ryan, R., & Frederick, C. (1997). On energy, personality, and health: Subjective vitality as a dynamic reflection of well-being. *Journal of Personality, 65*(3), 529–565.

Ryan, R., Deci, E., & Grolnick, W. (1995). Autonomy, relatedness, and the self: Their relation to development and psychopathology. In D. Cicchetti & D. Cohen (Eds.), *DevelopmentalPsychopathology* (pp. 618–655). New York, NY: Wiley.

Saldana, J. (2009). *The coding manual for qualitative researchers*. Thousand Oaks, CA: SAGE Publications, Inc.

Sangster, M. (2012). An fMRI study of sensory processing sensitivity. *Crossroads: An Undergraduate Research Journal of the Monmouth University Honors School*. 136-174. Retrieved from http://cms.monmouth.edu/uploadedFiles/Academics/Schools/Honors_

School/Crossroads2012.pdf#page=142

Schjolden, J., & Winberg, S. (2007). Genetically determined variation in stress responsiveness in rainbow trout: behavior and neurobiology. *Brain Behavior and Evolution, 70*(4), 227-238.

Seligman, M. (2006). *Learned optimism: How to change your mind and your life*. New York, NY: Random House.

Shifren, K. and Bauserman, R. (1996). The relationship between instrumental and expressive traits, health behaviors, and perceived physical health. *Sex Roles, 34*(11), 841-864.

Seidman, (2013). *Interviewing as qualitative research*. New York, NY: Teachers College Press.

Slater, P. (2009). *The chrysalis effect: The metamorphosis of global culture*. Portland, OR: Sussex Academic Press.

Smolewska, K., McCabe, S., Woody, E. (2006). A psychometric evaluation of the Highly Sensitive Person scale: The components of sensory-processing sensitivity and their relation to the BIS/BAS and "Big-Five." *Personality and Individual Differences, 40*(6), 1269–1297.

Storr, A. (1993). *The dynamics of creativity*. New York, NY: Random House.

Strelau, J. (1996). Individual differences in temperament: An international perspective. In J. Adair, D. Bélanger, & K. Dion (Eds.), *Advances in psychological science, Vol. 1: Social, personal, and cultural aspects* (pp. 33–51). Montréal, Canada: Psychology Press.

Strelau, J. (2009). *Psychologia temperamentu* [Psychology of temperament]. Warszawa: Wydawnictwo Naukowe PWN.

Strelau, J., & Zawadzki, B. (1993). The Formal Characteristics of Behavior-Temperament Inventory (FCB-TI): Theoretical assumptions and scale construction. *European Journal of Personality, 7*(5), 313–336.

Strelau, J., & Zawadzki, B. (1995). The Formal Characteristics of Behavior–Temperament Inventory (FCB-TI): Validity studies. *European Journal of Personality, 9*(3), 207–229.

Thomas, A., & Chess, S. (1977). *Temperament and development.* New York, NY: Brunner/Mazel.

Tupes, E., & Christal, R. (1961). *Recurrent personality factors based on trait ratings.* (Tech. Rep.). Lackland Air Force Base, TX: USAF.

Watkins, M., & Lorenz, H. (2002). Depth psychology and colonialism: Individuation, seeing-through, and liberation. In D. Slattery & L. Corbett (Eds), *Psychology at the threshold.* Carpinteria, CA: Pacifica Graduate Institute Publications.

Weissbluth, M. (1989). Sleep-loss stress and temperamental

difficultness:Psychobiological processes and practical considerations. InG. Kohnstamm, J. Bates, & M. Rothbart (Eds.), *Temperamentin childhood* (pp. 357-376). Chichester, England: Wiley.

Wiggins, J. S. (1968). Personality structure. *Annual Review of Psychology, 19*(1), 293–350.

Wilcock, A. (1993). A theory of the human need for occupation. *Occupational Science, 1*(1), 17-24.

Zeff, T. (2010). *The strong sensitive boy*. San Ramon, CA: Prana Publishing.

Zuckerman, M. (1979). *Sensation seeking: Beyond the optimal level of arousal*. Hillsdale, NJ: Lawrence Erlbaum Associates.

Zuckerman, M. (1983). *Biological bases of sensation seeking, impulsivity and anxiety*. Hillsdale, NJ: Lawrence Erlbaum Associates.

Zuckerman, M. (1991). *Psychobiology of personality*. Cambridge, England: Cambridge University Press.

Zuckerman, M., 2007. *Sensation seeking and risky behavior*. Washington, DC: American Psychological Association.

Zuckerman, M. (2009). Sensation seeking. In M. Leary and R. Hoyle (Eds.), *Handbook of individual differences in social behavior*. (pp. 455-465). New York, NY: The Guildford Press.

Appendix A: Participant Assessment Questionnaire

California Institute of Integral Studies

Tracy Cooper, a doctoral candidate at the California Institute of Integral Studies in San Francisco is conducting a research study to better understand the experiences of highly sensitive people in their search for a career that works for them.

Participation in this project is voluntary and no compensation is offered; however, you may find the experience to be enlightening and interesting. Your participation in this study will contribute significantly to our understanding of the needs of HSPs in the workplace. It is hoped this study will result in greater awareness of the unique needs of HSP's and also of their creative talents and abilities. This study will also serve as an entry point for the general public to become aware of the HSPs in their lives and the difficulties they face.

This form is intended to serve as an initial assessment to determine suitability and interest for the study. Please note that a blank or incomplete answer will not preclude you from participating. Your answers will ensure a broad cross section of HSPs are selected that reflect many backgrounds.

Please complete the following questions as fully as you are able. Before you begin please take the HSP self-test below. Be sure to enter a number, from 1-7 with 1 being not at all like you to 7 being extremely like you, in each space.

- What is your age? __ 18 – 29 __ 30 – 39 __ 40 – 49 __50 – 59 __60 – 69 __70 – 79 __80 - 89
- Do you live in an __urban, __suburban or __rural area?
- What country are you from?
- What is your highest level of education?
- What is your gender?

- Are you married, single, divorced, widowed?
- What is your current career?
- Do you work alone, in a team, or both?
- Are you willing to participate in an audio-recorded interview lasting 90 minutes conducted via Skype, in-person if possible, or telephone?
- How many careers have you had since age 18? __1 – 2 __3 – 5 __more than 5

Thank you for your answers and for your willingness to participate in this study. I will be in contact to set up the interview if selected.

Name:

Phone number:

Email address:

Skype Name:

Best day of the week for an interview:

Appendix B: HSP Self-Test

Instructions: Answer each question according to the way you personally feel. Check the box if it is at least somewhat true for you; leave unchecked if it is not very true or not at all true for you.

If you are a parent trying to evaluate your child, please use the test "Is Your Child Highly Sensitive?"

  ☐   I am easily overwhelmed by strong sensory input.

  ☐   I seem to be aware of subtleties in my environment.

  ☐   Other people's moods affect me.

  ☐   I tend to be very sensitive to pain.

  ☐   I find myself needing to withdraw during busy days,into bed or into a darkened room or any place where I can have some privacy and relief from stimulation.

  ☐   I am particularly sensitive to the effects of caffeine.

  ☐   I am easily overwhelmed by things like bright lights, strong smells,coarse fabrics,or sirens close by.

  ☐   I have a rich,complex inner life.

☐ I am made uncomfortable by loud noises.

☐ I am deeply moved by the arts or music.

☐ My nervous system sometimes feels so frazzled that I just have to go off by myself.

☐ I am conscientious.

☐ I startle easily.

☐ I get rattled when I have a lot to do in a short amount of time.

☐ When people are uncomfortable in a physical environment I tend to know what needs to be done to make it more comfortable (like changing the lighting or the seating).

☐ I am annoyed when people try to get me to do too many things at once.

☐ I try hard to avoid making mistakes or forgetting things.

☐ I make a point to avoid violent movies and TV shows.

☐ I become unpleasantly aroused when a lot is going on around me.

☐ Being very hungry creates a strong reaction in me,disrupting my concentration or mood.

☐ Changes in my life shake me up.

☐ I notice and enjoy delicate or fine scents, tastes, sounds, works of art.

☐ I find it unpleasant to have a lot going on at once.

☐ I make it a high priority to arrange my life to avoid upsetting or overwhelming situations.

☐ I am bothered by intense stimuli, like loud noises or chaotic scenes.

☐ When I must compete or be observed while performing a task, I become so nervous or shaky that I do much worse than I would otherwise.

☐ When I was a child, my parents or teachers seemed to see me as sensitive or shy.

Scoring:

If you answered more than fourteen of the questions as true of yourself, you are probably highly sensitive. But no psychological test is so accurate that an individual should base his or her life on it. We psychologists try to develop good questions, then decide on the cut off based on the average response.

If fewer questions are true of you, but extremely true, that might also justify calling you highly sensitive. Also, although there are as many men as women who are highly sensitive, when taking the test highly sensitive men answer slightly fewer items as true than do highly sensitive women.

Appendix C: CIIS Human Research Review Committee Approval Letter
California Institute of Integral Studies
Human Research Review Committee

December 3, 2013

Dear Tracy Cooper,

Congratulations, the Human Research Review Committee (HRRC) has approved your research proposal.

This approval is in effect for one year from the date of this letter. Any changes to your proposal from this point forward must be approved by the Committee in advance. It is understood that HRRC approval of your research does not imply endorsement by CIIS of any treatments, products, or theories associated with your research.

If you need more than one year to complete your research, you will need to apply for an extension to the HRRC before your one year expiration date. If this is needed, please submit in writing a statement of your request for extension and the reasons. You must also include a statement that no changes to your research have been made since this initial approval.

We wish you success with your research.

Sincerely,
Emi Kojima
HRRC Coordinator

cc: Michael Raffanti PhD/ mraffanti@ciis.edu

Appendix D: Participant Invitation

(to be posted in social media groups dedicated to HSPs)

I am conducting a study of highly sensitive persons and careers. The study will consist of one interview per participant lasting 90 minutes. All interview material is anonymous, your name will not be used in any resulting reports or future studies. If you are a self-described HSP and would like to participate please contact me at the email address below and I will send you more information. No financial incentive is offered for this study, but your participation will greatly aid me in better understanding how HSPs experience careers, the difficulties involved, and how you may have succeeded in finding a temperament-appropriate career.

Contact information: Tracy Cooper can be reached at tmcooper@socket.net.

Appendix E: Consent Form

California Institute of Integral Studies

Tracy Cooper, a doctoral candidate at the California Institute of Integral Studies in San Francisco, is conducting a research study into the lives of highly sensitive people and the difficulties they face finding careers that work for them given their personality trait.

Participation involves one audiotaped interview totaling 90 minutes. In the interview you will be asked a series of open-questions designed to learn about your experiences regarding your career/s. Some degree of reflection is recommended prior to the interview and I will email you some sample questions before the interview. Participation in this interview is based on self-identification as a highly sensitive person. There is a self-test you may take if you are in doubt. It is located at http://www.hsperson.com/pages/test.htm.

There are no risks involved in participating in this research beyond those experienced in everyday life. Some of the questions are personal and might cause discomfort. You will be free to refuse to answer any question or to end your participation in the study at any time. If you have any questions or concerns before or after the interview, Mr. Cooper will be available before, during, or after the interviewing process. He can be contacted at (660) 826-8969.

All information you contribute will be held in strict confidence within the limits of the law (see the attached confidentiality statement). The audiotapes and transcripts will be kept in a locked cabinet to which only Tracy Cooper has access. All identifying data will be deleted when direct quotes are used in the final report. Access to the recordings will be limited to Tracy Cooper.

The transcripts will be shared with you, if you wish, and

possibly Mr. Cooper's dissertation committee, Michael Raffanti, J.D., PhD., Joanne Gozawa, PhD., and Ted Zeff, PhD. Neither your name, your city, nor any other identifying information will be included in the final report. Your request to omit from the study particular details that you specify to the researcher will be honored. Tracy Cooper will also elicit from you other measures that you deem appropriate to further safeguard your confidentiality. The information you provide will be used in the final dissertation write-up and possibly in future publications.

No direct benefit, either monetary or resulting from the experience itself, is offered or guaranteed. You may, however, find the process interesting and thought-provoking. The information you provide will benefit the understanding of highly sensitive people, an often misunderstood group. If you have any concerns or questions regarding your rights as a participant in this research, or if you feel that you have been placed at risk, you may report them-- anonymously, if you wish-- to the Chair, Human Research Review Committee, California Institute of Integral Studies, 1453 Mission Street, San Francisco, CA 94103, telephone (415) 575-6100.

I, _____, consent to participate in the study of highly sensitive people and careers conducted by Tracy Cooper of the California Institute of Integral Studies. I have received a copy of this consent form and the Confidentiality Statement, and I understand that my confidentiality will be protected within the limits of the law.

_____

Signature   Date

If you would like to receive a written summary of the results of the study, please
provide an address where it can be sent to you.

_____

Street   City   Zip

Best time and date for an interview? _____ (please include

your time zone).

CONFIDENTIALITY STATEMENT

YOUR PRIVACY WITH RESPECT TO THE INFORMATION YOU
DISCLOSE DURING PARTICIPATION IN THIS STUDY WILL BE
PROTECTED WITHIN THE LIMITS OF THE LAW. NOTHING
WILL BE MADE PUBLIC THAT YOU WISH TO BE KEPT
PRIVATE.

Appendix F: Participant Bill of Rights

BILL OF RIGHTS
(FOR PARTICIPANTS IN PSYCHOLOGICAL RESEARCH)
You have the right to...
☐ ☐be treated with dignity and respect;
☐ ☐be given a clear description of the purpose of the study and what is expected of you as a
participant;
☐ ☐be told of any benefits or risks to you that can be expected from participating in the
study;
☐ ☐know the research psychologist's training and experience;
☐ ☐ask any questions you may have about the study;
☐ ☐decide to participate or not without any pressure from the researcher or his or her
assistants;
☐ ☐have your privacy protected within the limits of the law;
☐ ☐refuse to answer any research question, refuse to participate in any part of the study, or
withdraw from the study at any time without any negative effects to you;
☐ ☐be given a description of the overall results of the study upon request.
☐ ☐discuss any concerns or file a complaint about the study with the Human Research
Review Committee, California Institute of Integral Studies, 1453 Mission Street, San
Francisco, CA 94103.

FOR INDIVIDUALS WHO PARTICIPATE IN MEDICAL EXPERIMENTS
Persons who participate in a medical experiment are entitled to certain rights. These

rights include but are not limited to the subject's right to be informed of the nature and

purpose of the experiment; be given an explanation of the procedures to be followed in the

medical experiment and any drug or device to be utilized; be given a description of any

attendant discomforts and risks reasonably to be expected; be given an explanation of any

benefits to the subject, if applicable; be given a disclosure of any appropriate alternative,

drugs, or devices that might be advantageous to the subject and their relative risks and

benefits; be informed of the avenues of medical treatment, if any, available to the subject

after the experiment if complications should arise; be given an opportunity to ask questions

concerning the experiment or procedures involved; be instructed that consent to participate

in the medical experiment may be withdrawn at any time and that the subject may

discontinue participation without prejudice; be given a copy of the signed and dated consent

form; and be given the opportunity to decide to consent or not to consent to a medical

experiment without the intervention of any element of force, fraud, deceit, duress, coercion,

OR UNDUE INFLUENCE ON THE SUBJECT'S DECISION.

Appendix G: Sample Interview Questions to Participants

1. Can you tell me about your background?
   a. Where you are from?
   b. Where you grew up?
   c. How many people are in your family?
   d. Were your parents supportive of you?
2. What was your childhood like?
   a. Your school experience?
   b. What kind of interests did you have as a child?
   c. Did you know in some sense that you were a sensitive person?
3. What were you first experiences with work?
   a. What kinds of jobs did you have?
   b. What kinds of issues emerged in your first jobs if any?
   c. How did you envision having a career at that point in your life?
   d. In what ways has that vision changed now?
4. Can you tell me about each of the jobs you have had?
   a. What did you like about each one?
   b. What did you dislike about each one?
   c. Why did you decide to leave?
5. Looking back how do you feel being a HSP affected your choice of jobs?
   a. Has it been harder to find a job that works for you because of being a HSP?
   b. Has being a HSP been helpful in your working life? In what ways?
   c. What role did the physical working environment play for you?
   d. Were there any things about where you worked, like lights, cold/hot, cramped spaces that bothered you?

e. Were you affected by any interpersonal issues in your work? In what ways?
6. What kind of work do you like to do?
    a. What kinds of things matter to you in a job?
    b. What motivates you?
7. What role has being a highly sensitive male played for you?
    a. Has finding the right career been harder because you are a highly sensitive male? In what ways?
8. How are HSPs viewed in your culture?

Appendix H: Transcriptionist Confidentiality Statement

Subject: Confidentialty Statement

From   Starner, alicia M. 👤

To   tmcooper@socket.net 👤

Date   2013-12-10 10:20 am

Hello Tracy,
As requested I have read and agree to the confidentiality statement below.

I, Alicia Starner, agree to keep all information contained in the files I transcribe private and confidential. No information will be shared or discussed with anyone else or provided to any other source. Additionally, I agree to destroy all transcribed files upon receipt of confirmation of delivery and satisfactory condition from the study's author, Tracy Cooper.

Appendix I: Dissertation Committee

Michael Raffanti, PhD., J.D. CIIS Committee Chair.

Michael Raffanti, PhD., J.D. Dr. Raffanti's research interests include transdisciplinarity, grounded theory, transformative leadership, diversity dynamics, spirituality in organizations, systems change, anti-bias education, and human rights law. He holds a bachelor of arts in history and philosophy at the University of Portland, and Juris Doctor from Boston College Law School. He also holds a master's degree in teaching from The Evergreen State College where he focused on multicultural and anti-racist education and doctor of education degree from Fielding Graduate University. Dr. Raffanti became interested in an educational career while practicing poverty law in San Francisco. His involvement in developing a law academy at an urban high school precipitated his movement from law to education. He directed the education department of an AIDS service organization and developed HIV prevention programs for adolescents, gay and bisexual men, and communities of color. Dr. Raffanti taught Varieties of Scholarly Experience in the spring of 2012, and Basic Qualitative Research in the fall of 2012, both of which I participated in. In addition, I was Dr. Raffanti's doctoral teaching assistant for Varieties of Scholarly Experience in the spring of 2013 and 2014 and Basic Qualitative Research in the fall of 2013.

Dr. Raffanti can be reached at: The California Institute of Integral Studies, 1453 Mission Street San Francisco, California 94103, email: mraffanti@ciis.edu

Joanne Gozawa, PhD. Internal CIIS Committee Member.

Joanne Gozawa received her PhD in Integral Studies with a concentration in Learning and Change in Human Systems from CIIS in 2000. Prior to making teaching and academics her career, she was an organizational consultant focused on conflict and transformation.

Joanne's contribution to teaching and learning includes her transdisciplinary approach to inquiry. She asks about the dynamic synergy of the unconscious and the cultural and transpersonal dimensions of being that constitute the affective qualities of learning environments, including online ones. Joanne imagines these environments as subjects who are indifferent or who are caring about whether all who inhabit them actually learn. Learning environments that care, compel a deep listening attitude as a normative way to be. Learners take creative risks, engage diverse others, critically question personal beliefs and assumptions and are less discomforted by uncertainty when engaged in environments that care.

It is with sensitivity to the affective attributes of learning environments that Joanne is able to teach potentially provocative courses including ""Diversity in Action" and "Ways of Relating."

Joanne's overarching research question is, Why are both individual and systems unable to "reach across the aisle" to engage mutually in the throes of triggered emotions and conflict? She theorizes that adversaries' mutual vulnerability to existential dread is a contributing factor. Some of the ideas brought to bear on her inquiry are from the fields of consciousness studies, transformative learning, contemplative pedagogy, religion and evolution, Jungian psychology, moral psychology, myth and story, and Shin Buddhist thought. In addition she asks, how does computer mediated communication help or hinder provocation in learning? For this question she puts the aforementioned discourses in conversation with the field of online learning.

Dr. Gozawa can be reached at: The California Institute of Integral Studies, 1453 Mission Street San Francisco, California 94103, email: jgozawa@ciis.edu.

Ted Zeff, PhD. External Committee Member.

Ted Zeff, Ph.D., received his doctorate in psychology in 1981 from the California Institute of Integral Studies in San Francisco, CA. Dr. Zeff has more than 25 years of experience counseling sensitive children and adults. He currently teaches workshops and consults internationally on coping strategies for highly sensitive children and adults. Dr. Zeff is considered one of the world's experts on the trait of high sensitivity. He has given presentations and workshops in Denmark, The Netherlands and in many venues throughout the United States.

He is the author of *The Highly Sensitive Person's Survival Guide*, *The Highly Sensitive Person's Companion* and *The Strong, Sensitive Boy*. His books have been translated into five languages.

Dr. Zeff's articles about how to detect and prevent bullying have appeared in many magazines including Texas and Ohio State PTA, Canadian Association for Child and Play Therapy and the Connecticut School Psychologists Association He has been interviewed by Good Morning Bay Area on NBC TV, National Public Radio and Psychology Today, as well as by Dutch and Danish magazines.

Dr. Zeff can be reached at: tedzeff108@gmail.com.

Appendix J: High Sensation-Seeking Self-Test

Are You a Sensation Seeker?
A Self-Test
(reprinted from Aron, E., 2000, please see front matter, p. iv.)

Answer each question according to the way you feel. Answer true if it is at least somewhat true for you.

Answer false if it is not very true or not at all true for you.

T F If it were safe, I would like to take a drug that would cause me to have strange new experiences.

T F I can become almost painfully bored in some conversations.

T F I would rather go to a new place I may not like than go back again to a place I know I like.

T F I would like to try a sport that creates a physical thrill, like skiing, rock climbing, or surfing.

T F I get restless if I stay home for long.

T F I don't like waiting with nothing to do.

T F I rarely watch a movie more than once.

T F I enjoy the unfamiliar.

T F If I see something unusual, I will go out of my way to check it out.

T F I get bored spending time with the same people everyday.

T F My friends say it is hard to predict what I will want to do.

T F I like to explore a new area.

T F I avoid having a daily routine.

T F I am drawn to art that gives me an intense experience.

T F I like substances that make me feel "high."

T F I prefer friends who are unpredictable.

T F I look forward to being in a place that is new and strange to me.

T F To me, if I am spending the money to travel, the more foreign the country the better.

T F I would like to be an explorer.

T F I enjoy it when someone makes an unexpected sexual joke or comment that starts everyone laughing a little nervously.

Scoring the Sensation Seeker Self-Test

FOR WOMEN
If you answered true to 11 or more of the questions, you're probably a sensation seeker.
If you answered true to 7 or less of the questions, you are probably not a sensation seeker.
If you answered true to 8, 9, or 10 of the questions, you are probably somewhere in between on sensation seeking.

FOR MEN
If you answered true to 13 or more of the questions, you're probably a sensation seeker.
If you answered true to 9 or less of the questions, you are probably not a sensation seeker.
If you answered true to 10, 11, or 12 of the questions, you are probably somewhere in between on sensation seeking.

ABOUT THE AUTHOR

Dr. Tracy Cooper graduated from the California Institute of Integral Studies in 2014 with a Ph.D. in Integral Studies.

Dr. Cooper appeared in the documentary film *Sensitive–The Untold Story* and founded Invictus Publishing, llc in 2015 releasing *Thrill: The Highly Sensitive Person and Career*.

In 2016 he released *Thrill: The High Sensation Seeking Highly Sensitive Person.* In addition, his research findings connecting highly sensitive people to Dabrowski's Theory of Positive Disintegration were presented at the 2016 Dabrowski World Congress.

Continuing his focus on transdisciplinary research Dr. Cooper conducts ongoing new research with plans to publish *Tough: The Highly Sensitive Male, Re-Visioning Masculinity for the 21st Century* in 2017. He currently teaches at Baker University in a Master of Liberal Arts degree program and resides in Ozark, Missouri.

www.ingramcontent.com/pod-product-compliance
Lightning Source LLC
Chambersburg PA
CBHW030436290526
45786CB00001B/309